EBURY PRESS

THE MIRACLE MAKERS: INDIAN CRICKET'S GREATEST EPIC

Bharat Sundaresan is a world-renowned, award-winning cricket writer and commentator currently based in Adelaide, Australia. He is the Australian correspondent and senior writer for Cricbuzz, the No. 1 cricket website in the world, and also a commentator for SEN, the Melbourne-based sports radio station. He's the author of *The Dhoni Touch*, the 2018 national bestseller in India, which is considered the most in-depth biography of the Indian cricket superstar M.S. Dhoni, and *Believe*, which he co-wrote with Suresh Raina. Bharat is originally from Mumbai and worked for the *Indian Express*, a leading Indian national daily, covering cricket and other sports, for over 10.5 years, from May 2008 to December 2018. He has travelled to and covered tournaments in every major cricketing nation in the world. He has also written for several world-class publications around the world and appeared on numerous TV-news and current-affairs shows in Australia.

Gaurav Joshi has been a resident of Australia for thirty years. After working for ten years in IT, Gaurav decided to switch to sports journalism. For the past decade, Gaurav has freelanced as a writer and broadcaster for various media agencies, such as Fox Sports, Cricket Australia, *Mid-Day*, ABC, BBC and other cricket websites.

THE
MIRACLE
MAKERS

INDIAN CRICKET'S
GREATEST EPIC

BHARAT SUNDARESAN
with **GAURAV JOSHI**

EBURY
PRESS

An imprint of Penguin Random House

EBURY PRESS

USA | Canada | UK | Ireland | Australia
New Zealand | India | South Africa | China

Ebury Press is part of the Penguin Random House group of companies
whose addresses can be found at global.penguinrandomhouse.com

Published by Penguin Random House India Pvt. Ltd
4th Floor, Capital Tower 1, MG Road,
Gurugram 122 002, Haryana, India

Penguin
Random House
India

First published in Ebury Press by Penguin Random House India 2023

10 9 8 7 6 5 4 3 2 1

ISBN 9780143457497

Typeset in Bembo by MAP Systems, Bengaluru, India

www.penguin.co.in

To Australia, for accepting all of me, especially the cornucopia of colours, the chatter and the hair

Contents

1

Of Road Trips and Border Towns

I spent the night of 18 November 2020 at the Daydream Motel in Broken Hill. I'd driven there from Adelaide, after South Australia had ordered a lockdown at around 1 p.m. earlier that day. It meant that I had to cross over the border into New South Wales before midnight, which I managed to do with nine minutes to spare.

I was rather pleased with my great escape, having covered the 469 km in the dark of the night in my plush rental car, like I was in some sort of special-op scenario. In addition to the thrill of having pulled off this not-so-secretive mission, there was also the realization that I might have saved my summer of cricket.

'Isha, I really don't know when I'll be back. I really don't know what I'm getting into. Could be three weeks, a month, or two months.' These were my parting words to the wife as I picked up the Mitsubishi ASX from Adelaide Airport that evening. Maybe I was being a bit too dramatic, but at some level I was sincerely not sure what lay in store. But I honestly could not have ever envisaged just how the next two and a half months would play out.

In hindsight, I may have even undersold it to Isha. For, little did I know then that it would end up as the most incredible period of my journalistic career. Or that this would be only the first of many road trips I'd have to make. That this would be the first of many borders I'd have to flee across. That Broken Hill would be the first of many border towns that I'd have to sleep in. All to ensure that I could do justice to the most incredible cricket series of all time.

I was in good company for most of this span. Gaurav Joshi, that intrepid cricket nerd, was adventurous enough to not just stick with me through some tricky situations off the field, but he was also on hand to witness all the phenomenal on-field exploits—which ranged from the awe-inspiring to the jaw-dropping—from the best seat in the house, the one right next to mine.

My first destination back in November was in fact Gaurav's spacious and very welcoming home in the western part of Sydney. It was a 1200 km drive from Broken Hill, which should have taken me 12.5 hours to complete. If only he wouldn't have sent me well off the beaten track, suggesting a route that would eventually lead me into a part of central Australia which felt farther even than the back of beyond. Maybe because it was. No road, no cars, no people, not even a single kangaroo, and no phone signal. Only a dust track, the ASX and me.

It was the perfect introduction, though, to what I'd go on to refer to repeatedly as our 'Borders–Gavaskar Trophy' (used to be funny the first few times I mentioned it). By the time I got to the Joshi residence it was already 4 a.m. And the next morning, the first thing that was handed to me, along with my coffee, was a mask. This was peak pandemic after all. And while some of the states had held off the Covid virus quite successfully, it had broken through. So, while it was still a novelty for me to be walking around in a mask, Gaurav and the other Sydneysiders had been doing so for months already. It added to the uniqueness of the tour, along with the other niceties of having police personnel breathing over your neck as you watched the nets and having to stick cotton swabs up your nostrils on a regular basis.

The only reason I even had to drive halfway across the country to kick off my tour was because all the flights were running full. It took the guidance of Cricinfo ace, and my dear friend, Andrew McGlashan to enable me to take my first, of many, spot decisions by choosing to head off towards Sydney that night itself. It became a recurring theme, maybe even our routine: tune into the news at 12 p.m. to hear about the latest lockdown updates and find out which side of the state border we needed to get to by 12 a.m. that night.

We stuck to driving because it just seemed the safer option, even if it meant spending hours on end in the confines of a car. Not that Gaurav and I weren't used to doing that. We had, after all, spent a month and half in a campervan travelling all across England during the 2019 World Cup. Much more on that in a future book for sure.

Our first road trip in Australia together, which also included Isha, was in the direction of Melbourne but not quite all the way. It was the night after India's infamous batting collapse in Adelaide, when the three of us jumped into our car and headed to a farm close by, just beyond Bordertown—the actual name of the town bordering South Australia and Victoria. We then lay low there for a day before driving to Melbourne and finding a drive-in Covid testing centre on the outskirts—the only one open at that hour and not queued up for 3–4 km. Yes, that was part of the fun too.

The uncertainty that gripped everyone over the latter half of the Test series led to further confusion. It led Gaurav and me into a stakeout-like situation in . . . where else but another motel, this time in Wodonga, on the Victorian side of the border it shares with New South Wales (NSW). Considering we were well in the know about the apprehensions of the Indian cricket team management about going into a tighter bubble with more restrictions in Sydney, we thought it best to wait till we'd heard that their flight had taken off from Melbourne before driving up the 3 km to cross into NSW.

Of course, we had our own contingency plans if there was to be any last-minute drama. Robbie MacKinley, a friend of ours from Albury—the border town on the NSW side—was all set to take us to this hidden spot, from where we could have swum across the Murray River back into Victoria. Yeah, this was seriously considered as an option too. As you'll read further in the book, this wasn't even the most dangerous of activities we indulged in to get a bit closer to the action.

Speaking of which, Gaurav had spent the first few days of the tour avoiding cops and security guards around Blacktown Oval to find a vantage point from where we could watch India's early training sessions. In fact, even as I was trying to find my way back to civilization on my drive to Sydney, I was on the phone with him—whenever possible—hearing about the 'different' plans that Team India seemed to have brought to these shores this time around. You will read about all this, as well as about the men who'd planned it, the coaching staff and those who executed it— the array of superstars that India found along the way.

Our interactions with the players were different in their own way. While they were in bubbles, we would still bump into them, and we were, for many of them, the major source of information in regard to the ground reality of the Covid situation in Australia.

While we had enough access to them at practice, and even at times during the matches, we were completely cut off when it came to actual media interactions. This was also when we were introduced to the epoch-defining concept of the Zoom call.

On a sidenote, the first time I heard the term 'Covid' mentioned was courtesy of an Indian cricketer. It was in Hamilton earlier that year, when I'd overheard Washington Sundar innocently asking the team manager about it. Washington would later emerge as a breakout star on this tour. He was but only one of the many young Indians who'd arrived here in the midst of a pandemic, hoping to create an impression on Australia, and left an indelible mark on the cricketing world that Australians will talk about for years to come.

Every time this relentless Indian team felt like a door had been shut on them, another opened and out walked a hero. And that probably would be the lasting legacy of this, at times, unbelievable achievement by India's miracle men, amid all the majestic performances, the shocking reversals, the courageous comebacks and the eventual glory.

In addition to reporting on the cricket for Cricbuzz, I was also privileged enough to be doing radio commentary on the Test series for the Australian radio station SEN. And that gave me the chance to witness this cricketing feat from a unique perspective. I witnessed first-hand how some of the greats in Australian cricket were left awe-struck by this Indian team's unflappable spirit. I saw the mighty Australians acknowledge them with the same veneration that generations of Indians had felt for Australian cricketers.

Eventually, the borders caught up with Gaurav and me. Our decision to head to Sydney for the third Test ruled out any possibility of our getting to the Gabba. Still, I was fortunate enough to be on radio from the Sydney studios and to be on air when Rishabh Pant hit that boundary to complete India's greatest-ever Test series win.

It didn't mean I could simply roll back home, though. South Australia (SA) had shut its borders to New South Wales. And I was told, in no uncertain terms, by SA Health that my best option was to 'drive around regional NSW for two weeks' before being allowed back into South Australia. So that's what I did. I was fortunate to start my expedition with two wonderful nights in the beautiful town of Orange, hosted by the equally wonderful Melinda Farrell.

From there on, I spent one night each in various country towns of all shapes and sizes, from Dubbo and Canowindra to Forbes and Wilcannia, and made day trips to every 'historical' site in between, including one to the lovely Jelissa Apps's hometown of Booroowa, before a final pit stop back at where it had all started. By that time, of course, the Indian team had returned home and had already begun their next series against England.

On 5 February 2021, I returned to Daydream Motel in Broken Hill. By then, I'd covered around 5000 km across the length and breadth of central and eastern Australia. I'd stayed in more border towns and driven past more borders than I'd ever imagined. By then, I'd also seen more of regional Australia than I knew existed. But most importantly, I'd also had the privilege of covering a memorable, if not era-defining, tour in cricket history that will never be matched or replicated.

2

Bubbling Away

'This will be the most unique tour since the Second World War.'

'I've told the boys suck it up for fourteen days. It might feel like a prison, but after that you will be free birds.'

Those were pretty much the first two lines Ravi Shastri said to us and, in all probability, to his team as well, right after India landed in Sydney on 12 November 2020.

The Pullman Hotel at Sydney Olympic Park resembled a high-security complex on a warm November evening. Tall barricades were erected around the hotel entrance. Two police cars were stationed at the top of the road leading to the hotel. One lane was blocked with fleet barricades to ensure no cars could manoeuvre their way to the hotel driveway. Two more police vehicles waited at the main junction to escort the buses into the dedicated parking area in front of the lobby. Private security guards were also present for the smooth transition of the players from the bus to the reception area.

'What is happening here? Why are there so many police cars and barricades?' a lady passing by asked Gaurav.

The Sydney Olympic Park area, where Gaurav had worked as a volunteer during the 2000 Olympics, consists of multiple sporting fields and stadiums. There are a few offices, a gym and a couple of residential blocks as well. Unless there is a sporting event in progress, the area is generally very quiet and passive. So, it was only understandable that some of the residents returning from work were a little concerned about this heavy security presence.

Not many seemed amused or pleased with this change of scenery. Certainly not the lady who'd checked with Gaurav. She even had a pretty pointed lament: 'Seriously, the things we do for sportsmen in this country is remarkable. We have Australians stranded abroad and they can't get home because our borders are closed. And here is our government making exemptions for some sporting matches—it is ridiculous.' Clearly not a cricket fan.

The Australian government had shut the international borders in March 2020. Even Australian citizens and permanent residents were subject to quota limits for travel and, on their return home, a mandatory fourteen-day quarantine period in a hotel at their own expense. At the time of the Indian team's arrival, close to 30,000 Australians were still waiting to get back home with no guarantees as to when. So for someone to be displeased about the exemption granted to the Indian team and the Australian players returning from the Indian Premier League (IPL) was very understandable.

Twenty-four hours prior to the team's arrival, Gaurav had decided to scope the hotel out. It helped that it was only a twenty-minute drive from his house. The minute he arrived, though, he was turned away by a security guard. Gaurav was informed that the hotel had been vacated and the rooms sanitized. At that point, the hotel staff were in the process of sealing the entrance from the outside. Further attempts were made to snoop around a bit more and engage the hotel management staff so they would give us an overview of the protocols in place. But we were kindly informed that since it was a state government matter, no details could be provided.

The only information that could be gathered through the reconnaissance mission came from a security guard. 'We have strict instructions that no one from outside the barricades can enter the hotel space. All the staff are in a bubble and cannot mix with anyone. Mate, even the people inside have been isolating for the last day or two. They can't go home for the next fourteen days either.'

If we didn't know it already, it was clear that this was going to be no ordinary cricket tour. But this was our first glimpse into just how different it was going to be. After receiving special permission from the New South Wales government to quarantine the Australian players returning from the IPL and the Indian team in Sydney, Cricket Australia (CA) had to first decide on a hotel where they could accommodate the players for those first two weeks. In a normal world, visiting teams are put up in a five-star hotel in the Sydney CBD around the scenic harbour. But after a couple of meetings between CA and the state government, it was decided that a remote location within the confines of the Sydney Olympic Park (20 km from the Sydney CBD) would be the ideal choice.

CA had already successfully created a 'soft' bubble at the Novotel across the road from the Pullman for the WBBL teams. And eventually, while Gaurav and I were waiting outside the hotel for the Indian players to leave and get on the bus, we did spot a few of the WBBL players in a much looser bubble on the other side of the quiet road.

The secluded location, and the fact that CA were able to completely book the hotel for the Indian and Australian teams, made it the most viable option. It meant that from 12–26 November, nobody but the players, coaches and their families would be permitted to live at or visit the property. It was also learnt that the Indian team ideally wanted a facility to train at during the fourteen-day quarantine period.

'We were going to play an ODI match a day after the fourteen days of isolation. How can we play the game if all the players have been sitting in their rooms for two weeks? We demanded to have access to training and a gym,' one of the coaches would tell us very early on during the tour.

Initially, it was decided that the Cricket NSW office adjacent to the Pullman would provide the Indian players with facilities such as indoor nets and a gym. However, conducting indoor practice sessions for a long period of time was considered a 'risk' under Covid protocols. Also, trying to mix the Indian players up in a small section of the NSW cricket offices posed a challenge. So a decision was made to conduct all the practice sessions during that fourteen-day period at the Blacktown International Stadium (35 km from Sydney city and 20 km from the Pullman). The gymnasium equipment would be transported to the ground and set up at these special premises at Blacktown Oval.

The Emirates' chartered flight from Dubai touched down in Sydney at 6 p.m. on 12 November. All the players and staff on board exited the airport from a VIP gate, a rare treat in Australia. Members of the Australian Army were present to guide them and load the baggage on to the various buses.

There was a police escort in place from the airport to the hotel. The Australian players returning from the IPL arrived first. Each of them was taken inside by security personnel. The tall barricades made it difficult for those outside to even get a view of the players as they disembarked from the bus. Gaurav wasn't the only person of Indian origin trying to look through the barricades, of course. And it wasn't his first time waiting outside Sydney Airport to steal a glance at a visiting Indian team either.

The Indian team arrived in four different buses. Due to social distancing measures, only fourteen people were allowed on each bus. Masks were still compulsory on board, and the driver had a plastic shield around his seat to ensure there was no contact with any of the visitors.

The Indian team, including the support staff and families, comprised over fifty personnel. It took close to thirty minutes for all the members to enter the hotel. It was a slow, tedious process, as only one bus got unloaded at a time, while the second bus waited in the police-guarded parking space.

It was difficult to recognize some of the players with masks and sunglasses covering their faces. The one man missing was Rohit Sharma, who, despite the mask and glasses, would have been difficult to miss, thanks to his unique gait and body language.

Once everyone had entered the hotel, a large van, carrying all the kits, arrived. The army troops assisted in unloading the bags. All that luggage needed to be sanitized before being passed on to each player or stored in a separate room. The whole process must have taken at least 4–5 hours, and, to his credit, Gaurav hung in there, noticing whatever he could.

Later that evening, we both received phone calls from Ravi Shastri, who sounded very happy to be back in Australia, even if it was in these unprecedented circumstances, and was also chuffed with how the team had been treated upon arrival. 'We are extremely happy with the way they have looked after us since we landed. The way the team was escorted from the plane, through customs and then on to the bus, was extremely professional. No fuss and well-organized,' he said.

The Indian team management was also keen on understanding the politics between the states in Australia, in terms of questions like: Why are they closing state borders? Why can't the central government have a say on how a particular state deals with its borders? Who is Peta Credlin? We tried our best to describe the political geography of the land. But we still found ourselves reiterating the point that moving between some states was not possible. Finally, I decided to explain it with an Indian reference. 'It's like if Maharashtra and West Bengal had the powers to stop people from travelling from one state to the other, with the Modi government unable to do anything about it.'

Some of them also wanted to know why Queensland was so pedantic about their border closures. We were told that one of the discussions between CA and the Indian team had led to the possibility of the teams being housed in a prestigious boarding school in Brisbane, where they could train on the school ovals.

Whatever the case was, the message from the visitors was loud and clear from the very start: 'We will not be locked up inside for the first fourteen days, and we will not be confined to any place after those first fourteen days.'

The players and staff were then given a rundown as to the dos and don'ts while inside the hotel. The protocols were extremely strict. Most of the players were flabbergasted to learn that they could not even visit each other in their respective rooms. If a player needed to visit the physio or doctor, it had to be in a common space, with only two people allowed. Apart from a medical emergency, there was to be very limited interaction between the support staff and players. At some quarantine facilities, the food would be left outside their doors, with wooden cutlery. The players travelling with kids—Cheteshwar Pujara, Ajinkya Rahane and R. Ashwin—were, thankfully, given slightly bigger rooms.

There was an Indian chef permanently stationed inside the hotel, but we were told that Indian food was the kind typically found overseas, or *goren logon ka Indian khana*, as one of them put it—butter chicken or some 'curry'. A few of the players immediately ask if Uber Eats was allowed and started ordering away. But there was always a delay with every order, since the food packets needed to be sanitized every time they arrived.

The Indian contingent was immediately tested for Covid on the night of arrival. They would be allowed outside only once they had tested negative. Each individual was to be tested a minimum of three times before the fourteen-day period ended.

The only time the players were allowed outside the hotel was to attend training sessions at Blacktown. The wives and kids of the players could not even exit their hotel rooms for those fourteen days. Two police officers were stationed on each floor to ensure that all the protocols were followed.

The team management had also advised the players to follow every stringent health-and-safety protocol diligently without any slip-ups, to ensure that they were in a position to move around a bit more freely once the quarantine period concluded.

'Basically, we have to treat each person as if they are Covid positive. All of us working in the hotel cannot leave here until the fourteen-day period is finished,' one of the hotel staff told us.

It was decided that the team would not train for the first couple of days. However, the media manager of the team let us know the change of plan the very next day. What had happened was that the team had decided to advance their training by a day, because all of them had agreed on a Zoom call that there was no point sitting inside the hotel room. The healthier option was to travel to Blacktown. This would enable the players to be outdoors for 3–4 hours. Plus, they could interact in person with each other and get some fresh air.

The players were told no food could be taken from the hotel to the ground, so fruits and snacks needed to be sanitized and carried by the support staff.

The players were constantly reminded by the coaching staff that this would be the hardest period of the tour. After a fourteen-hour flight to Sydney, which has a seven-hour time difference with the UAE, where all of them had come from, they were heavily jet-lagged. The majority of the players had become accustomed to living inside the bubble during the IPL, but the protocols in Australia were harder to adapt to.

One of them said, 'It's already harder than Dubai, with no balcony, and the sunny weather makes it hard for us to digest the fact that we cannot enjoy the outdoors, especially in Australia. So I just decided to keep the curtains closed.' Another player missed his breakfast because he didn't hear the knock on the door. He was told that the food could only be left at his doorstep for a certain time.

One player recalled, 'The only thing that was exciting was the huge storm that hit the hotel. I was so bored that I literally watched the clouds build up and then the rain. Great day for Insta stories and catching up on sleep. What else can we do?'

After a few days of bubble life, some of the players were more frustrated than others, while several had forged a routine. 'We would leave the hotel around twelve and be back around five or six. When we got back, we would refresh, eat, spend time chatting with our family or catch up with people back home in India. The night-time was ideal to catch up with friends back home, as it was late afternoon in India. We would head to bed past midnight, and by the time we woke up, it was time for breakfast, and then we headed off to practice. This routine ensured we remained sorted and helped us get over jet lag quite soon,' a player recently told me.

Since the players were not allowed to use the gym inside the hotel, they had to use the fitness equipment that was transported and set up in a marquee at the Blacktown facility adjacent to the training ground. The equipment could be used by multiple players, and a couple of support staff members were allowed inside the marquee at one time.

CA had done a fantastic job providing all the facilities outdoors. But some of the players were still confused about the regulations.

'I'm getting another player to help me with bench-press or weight drills. We are sweating and sharing equipment, but we can't go into each other's hotel rooms. We are permitted to be outdoors without masks. I don't get it,' a player said.

Exiting their rooms to board the bus for the training session was also an irksome journey. Only four players were allowed in the elevator at a time, meaning each member had to follow a sequence of when they could exit their room to walk down the corridor to the lift.

'It reminded me of school, where they would call out a class or a name, and only then you could go. Luckily, they didn't ask us to hold our hands and walk in a straight line,' said a senior player.

A police escort was required in the front and back of the bus for the 20-km journey to the training facility. Rather than for safety or security reasons, the purpose of the police escorts in the bus was to ensure that the bubble was not breached by anyone outside under any circumstances.

A member of the CA logistics team would explain later the detailed nature of the transportation plans. 'We had to cover every possibility, like a breakdown or even an accident, with a member needing to be transported elsewhere. It had to be done without breaching the bubble. We simply could not take any risk. One breach and there would be uproar from the public and the possibility of the tour being cancelled. For us, those fourteen days were so critical.'

Perhaps the most arduous phase during the fourteen-day span were the few days of Diwali. Around that time, the Board of Control for Cricket in India (BCCI) had tried to create a small window where the players could return home if they were playing in India or at least get together as a team for dinner or a celebration. However, on this occasion they had to stay put inside their rooms and wish each other on video calls, despite being literally 50 m away.

'I was lucky to have my immediate family in the room, but for a lot of the players they were away, and they couldn't even say "Happy Diwali" to each other or give each other a hug or enjoy a sneaky sweet,' one of them told us.

A couple of players inquired if there was any possibility for them to access any Diwali sweets. Well, there was never any dearth of sweets or generosity in the Joshi household. So Gaurav volunteered to go and drop off some home-made traditional sweets for some of the players.

When Gaurav later asked one of them if he had tasted the sweets, the reply was, 'Thanks, but no thanks. This is a long tour, and I don't know when my opportunity will arise. I may have to wait until the last game, and if I eat a cheat meal/sweet now, I will be doing injustice to my body and fitness regimen.' As we'll find out in a later chapter, these words from this particular player would prove to be prophetic.

It wasn't just the Indian players who were craving for some special food; a few of the Sydney-based Australian players had their partners/wives deliver food to them from their favourite local joints.

While the players tried their best to get accustomed to the bubble life, they continued to probe us about the protocols at the end of the fourteen-day period. 'Do you know if we will be allowed to move around after the quarantine period?' 'How many cases are there today in Sydney?' If there are so little, surely we can roam out?' 'Surely, the purpose of this quarantine is to ensure we can move around in the public like others in Sydney?' These were but some of the questions popping up on our phones rather regularly. You couldn't help but feel for them.

CA, meanwhile, was pleased with having managed to come up with a 'best-case' scenario, alongside the New South Wales government, for the Indian team. 'We want the Indians to enjoy rather than have them endure this tour over the next two months' was a line you heard from many in their logistics team.

There was some relief, too. Many believed that if the tour had started in Queensland, which seemed very likely for a long while before Sydney entered the fray, the protocols might have been stricter.

A few days into the hard lockdown, it still remained unclear just how free the Indian players, coaches and families would be to move around the cities once it was eased. The only certainty was that they'd shift to a hotel closer to the city the day they were out of quarantine. Not surprisingly, most of the players and coaches had packed up and were ready a few hours before they had to board the bus that would take them into the city on 26 November.

'At least we will get the Sydney Harbour views and see the city skyline. After five days in this hotel, this view is getting boring. At least in Dubai, during the IPL, we had some nice views of the water. The room was also so much bigger and had a treadmill or some gym equipment,' a player said about their upcoming move to the Harbour Esplanade.

At some point during those initial two weeks, the then interim CEO of CA, Nick Hockley, had explained the measures that could be in place once the Indians had left the Pullman. 'We need to clearly make sure that from a biosecurity perspective, we are minimizing the risk. That said, at this time, Australia is very fortunate to be one of the safest places in the world. So, once they're clear through their quarantine, we've got measures in place which are risk-weighted to ensure that everyone is kept safe, but players will enjoy a level of freedom in Australia, and those are very well documented between CA and the BCCI,' Hockley said. The Indian team management, too, was confident that they would be allowed to move about more freely once the series was officially under way. But it wasn't to be.

They were soon informed that there would be restrictions similar to those that the players in the Sheffield Shield hub in Adelaide had to contend with. That would mean being able to get takeaways and even dining in at venues which provide outdoor seating, but not being able to enter cafés, restaurants and pubs.

'I'm mentally exhausted. I just wanted to sit at least on a balcony with fresh air and have a coffee. Feel like just going and training all day, so then I can tire myself out and just sleep,' a player informed us. The quarantine was getting to a lot of them.

While the first Sydney leg of the tour began to take some definite shape, the logistics of the Indian team's travels to other states, especially to Adelaide, the venue of the first Test, remained uncertain.

Adelaide's sudden spike in new Covid-19 cases had already seen Western Australia (WA), Queensland and Tasmania either shut their borders with South Australia or have all visitors from the state undergo self-isolation for fourteen days. It resulted in state cricketers from Tasmania and WA in particular, who had returned home from the Sheffield Shield in Adelaide, being forced to quarantine at their respective homes for two weeks. They included Test skipper Tim Paine, along with Matthew Wade, Cameron Green and white-ball spinner Ashton Agar.

The bigger issue for CA seemed to be finding a way of getting the likes of Green and Agar to Sydney in time for the opening ODI at the Sydney Cricket Ground (SCG) on 27 November.

The sanctions imposed by the South Australian government meant CA had to deviate from the original plan of assembling all the Australian players in Adelaide and instead shift the first Test itself to Sydney. Within a few hours, Paine and coach Justin Langer were on a flight to Sydney. We still hadn't had any cricket yet, but there was already a lot happening on this tour.

The rapid escalation of the situation in South Australia prompted a member of the Indian team management to say jokingly, 'Looks like no city wants to host us? Do the Aussies really want to play against us or what?'

Another player had begun insisting that the Adelaide Test was in jeopardy. 'Will they shift the Adelaide Test now? I saw the news that there are cases. How many?' When informed that the total number was six, there was a pause at the other end of the call, a deep breath and, 'That's just incredible. They shut down the city with six new cases? Most households in India have six positive cases.'

The lack of socialization was affecting the younger players most.

'How much Netflix and Amazon can you watch. We were in the IPL bubble for two months, and before that most cities were in a hard lockdown for six months. Is there anything interesting on Australian TV?' one player said.

Gaurav even managed to convince one of them to give the Rugby League a go. It so happened that the final game of the three-match State of Origin series was being broadcast on Channel 9 that evening. For the uninitiated, the State of Origin is to New South Wales and Queensland what an India vs Pakistan cricket match is for these two countries. You have to live through it in Australia to realize that my statement isn't as blasphemous as it may sound.

The game was played in Brisbane and drew a capacity crowd of 50,000. The sight of spectators at a sporting event in Australia prompted one cricketer to ask, 'How can there be people at the stadium? It seems packed. Aren't there cases and lockdowns in Australia?'

At some point, we realized that the best way to deal with it was to just listen to them and let them vent out. We did, however, tell them that the rugby match was played in Brisbane, where there were no Covid cases, largely due to the fact that the state had closed its borders to any state with 'one or more' Covid cases in the last six months.

Over in Adelaide, it was still not clear whether Virat Kohli & Co. would be staying at the Adelaide Oval Hotel, which had opened in September 2020 and already housed a few of the Australian players who'd returned from the tour of England. There were also more cricketing issues, like if net bowlers had to be arranged by the South Australian Cricket Association for the visitors.

While CA worked around the clock to ensure they didn't have to rework their original schedule any more than they already had, the Indian team continued with their hard lockdown. With each passing day, the players knew they were closer to achieving some sort of freedom. At the same time, the team continued to train hard and conjure up plans for the month and a half ahead.

On the thirteenth day of quarantine, the team were told that they would be relocated to a hotel in the city. But it came with a disclaimer, that there wouldn't be complete freedom for them. 'We can't pose for selfies or autographs. We have to avoid crowded places and no indoor seating. We can't travel by Uber either,' was how one player summed up the rules.

Each member had to return a negative test on the fourteenth day to exit quarantine. Finally, on 26 November, it was time to leave the Pullman. The official transition from a 'hard' bubble to a 'softer' bubble wasn't going to happen till they reached their new accommodation. So, the exit procedure was to be as lengthy as the entry procedure was. Only that by now, Indian fans in this part of Sydney had identified the hotel in which the team had been staying for the past fourteen days.

At 5 p.m. on Freedom-from-Quarantine Day, a contingent of thirty fans had gathered outside the hotel to get a glimpse of the players. The presence of the police and the barriers on either side of the bus parked right outside the hotel entrance had already caused quite a stir. But the dozen excitable Indians pointing their phones in that direction added to the curiosity in the neighbourhood again.

'Has something happened to someone in there?' a lady asked the handful of policemen outside the posh hotel with genuine concern. Another woman actually pulled her car by the kerb and rolled her window down to inquire if 'someone important' was about to emerge through the doors of the hotel.

A young Pakistan fan, not older than twelve, chose this to be the perfect chance for some cross-border fun. 'Pakistan is a better team! *Dil, dil,* Pakistan!' he screamed and sang, but ran off before the Indian fans present could react.

Virat Kohli even flashed a thumbs-up sign before placing his bags in the luggage compartment and boarding the bus. He was, of course, serenaded with a few chants while he did so.

The quarantine shackles had been taken off. The players would no longer be completely confined again—or so they thought. You could sense that they had been waiting to be out and about. Later that evening, most of the players were spotted walking around the Sydney Opera House and Sydney Harbour. Some still continued to wear masks outdoors, while others soaked in the fresh air mask-free.

A player inquired if they were permitted on a ferry ride on the harbour, only to be told 'no', since this counted as public transport. Players with families visited the Botanical Gardens adjacent to the hotel.

A bunch of the younger lot was spotted in a flashy convertible with some locals, with loud Punjabi music booming out. When a senior player was told about this scene, he simply shook his head and said, 'This new generation *bindaas hai re* (This new generation is fearless).'

While driving home, Gaurav's car was mistaken for an Uber by a few white-ball players out for a long walk. Maybe the 'not being allowed to travel in an Uber' protocol had slipped past them. Another player said 'Sorry, *bhai*' before asking Gaurav what the shortest path back to their hotel was.

Another senior member was busy pushing a stroller up the steep slope from the harbour to the hotel. Recognizing us, he stopped to chat and revealed that this was his family's final night on the tour. 'They are going back tomorrow. I wanted them with me during the fourteen-day period. We were glad to have the families during that time. Now it's back to business.'

A few days later, I bumped into K.L. Rahul and Mayank Agarwal by the Sydney Opera House. They still couldn't get why there was no freedom, especially when there were so few cases in Australia. You tried explaining it to them. They nodded, but you could make out they were not convinced.

A few days later, though, Virat Kohli got it: 'It's because you guys have such a good system here, and because people follow the rules, that Australia has managed to control the pandemic so well. I totally get why we aren't getting to go out much.'

3

Will They? Won't They?

'Will you be coming to IPL?'

This was the message that we received from more than a couple of players from India's Test and ODI teams in the first week of September 2020.

When informed that we couldn't do that since Australia's international borders were shut and nobody could travel in or out of the country, pat came the next question: 'Then how would the Australia tour take place?'

I'm not suggesting that any of them wasn't keen on seeing Gaurav or me landing up in the UAE for the IPL. But we realized pretty early on that these messages had more to do with the uncertainty and confusion surrounding their trips to our part of the world. And when one of them was informed about how Cricket Australia was forging plans with state governments and trying every avenue available to get the Indian cricketers to come to Australia, he found it rather amusing. Not so much the bit about the hardships in even getting this tour started, but the fact that we had more information than he did. 'You have more updates than we do. Nobody has said anything to us thus far.'

By that time, the majority of the players had already entered the IPL bubble in Dubai. Those expecting to be in the three squads for Australia had also packed and prepped to not return home before late January—if they were especially in plans for the Test team.

Those who were not part of an IPL franchise were still at home in India, fighting the same doubts. There was also that other big question of whether they would be permitted to take their families along.

On the other hand, CA were yet to get an official confirmation of the tour taking place from the BCCI, and that meant that their plans to confirm the tour remained in limbo. Australia's international borders still remained tightly shut, and Virat Kohli's team would require a special government approval to enter the country.

As we learnt in the previous chapter, a fifty-eight-strong Indian contingent did land in Sydney on 12 November 2020, kicking off one of the most surreal cricket tours of all time. While as miraculous as some of the performances and events that transpired over the following two and a bit months were, getting the tour sorted in the wake of the deadliest pandemic the world had seen in over a century seemed in itself like something that required a miracle. And those who did make it happen in both countries deserve a lot of plaudits and sympathy in equal measure.

It all started with an email exchange between the BCCI and CA, which happened as early as April 2020, but nothing was set in concrete. This was when the world was still coming to grips with the Covid virus having taken over its reins.

Around the same time, reports began to emerge in the Australian media about the financial loses CA had incurred. An article in *Guardian Australia* stated, 'In 2016, at the start of the cycle, CA had cash and investments worth about $270 million—that figure had dropped to about $97 million in March 2020.'

Now there was an added significance to that Indian tour. So much so that some feared that the future of Australian cricket depended on Kohli & Co. agreeing to play and then flying to these shores. Not to forget, it was also a matter of their being allowed to enter Australia.

Early reports suggested that the tour would be worth around A$300 million, enough to save the day for CA. The man most under the pump was the then CEO, Kevin Roberts. To make matters worse, Roberts and CA had made the sensational decision to furlough 200 staff on just 20 per cent pay in March 2020.[1] The CA board and the states were at loggerheads, and the Australian Cricketers' Association (ACA) was also demanding answers.[2] The heat was on, and Roberts and CA had to fight fires in all directions, facing the media almost once every two days, and with no answers yet from India.

In late April, Kevin Roberts, chief of CA, stated in a press conference that there was 90 per cent chance that India's tour would take place. Roberts also confirmed that CA would consider housing Indian players and support staff at a 'quarantine hub' such as Adelaide Oval's yet-to-be-completed 128-room hotel, where Kohli's squad could remain to train and play during the Test campaign without the need for additional travel.

I, for one, wasn't complaining about the prospect of four home Tests to be honest. But one knew even then that Sydney and Melbourne would never let CA get away with it, pandemic or no pandemic. The ramifications of India not coming were being projected to be so dire that some reports even suggested that Australian cricket might end up close to 'bankruptcy'.

The BCCI had their own 'closer-to-home' issues to deal with. And when an Australian journalist contacted them for an update on the tour around May, he was told that the BCCI was only focusing on seeing how to pull off the IPL at that point and that the Australian tour was yet to be discussed.

To make it harder, the broadcasters were also pushing CA for a confirmation, as they needed to map out their schedule and work

---

[1] https://www.smh.com.au/sport/cricket/savage-cuts-save-cricket-only-3m-as-states-question-cash-crisis-20200420-p54lks.html; https://www.smh.com.au/sport/cricket/anatomy-of-a-fall-inside-the-demise-of-cricket-australia-chief-kevin-roberts-20200618-p5543f.html

[2] https://www.theguardian.com/sport/2020/apr/21/cricket-australia-could-lose-hundreds-of-millions-of-dollars-in-coronavirus-crisis

out the logistics. With the official fixture date release getting closer, there was still no confirmation. CA started to panic. One of them had received a text message containing nothing but a 'thumbs up' emoji from a higher-up in the Indian board. Would that count as an approval, one good enough to go ahead and announce the tour?

While the wait continued, the date to release the fixtures arrived. Chairman Earl Eddings did make a desperate bid to receive a last-minute official confirmation, but at the end CA ended up trusting the BCCI and announced the fixtures, stating that the first Test against India will start at the Gabba on 3 December.

A senior CA official then received a call from his counterpart in India; the latter wondered how CA had gone ahead with the announcement without having heard back from them. Satisfied with the response, he did give an assurance that the players were looking forward to touring. No official confirmation yet, though.

On 16 June, Roberts was sacked, and Nick Hockley was appointed as interim boss of Cricket Australia. The tour was still on, but as Covid continued to create havoc around the world, the T20 World Cup scheduled in Australia was now under serious threat. In July, the International Cricket Council (ICC) made the decision to postpone the world event that was to begin in October. Doubts resurfaced once again over whether India would arrive on these shores as per schedule, especially with the Australian border still under a hard lockdown and cases beginning to rise all around the country except South Australia. Melbourne had already gone into a lockdown.

However, later that week, BCCI president Sourav Ganguly confirmed to an Indian news channel that the national team would definitely be touring Australia. But it came with a disclaimer. 'Yes, we have confirmed that tour. In December we will be coming. We just hope the number of quarantine days gets reduced a bit. Because we don't want the players to go all that far and sit in hotel rooms for two weeks. It is very, very depressing and disappointing,' Ganguly told the TV channel *India Today*.

Meanwhile, the BCCI confirmed that IPL 2020, which had been postponed from its original schedule of April and May, would be conducted behind closed doors in the UAE from 19 September to 10 November. That only meant more anxiety for CA. Another spanner in the works. While they wanted to ensure that all their players would participate in the IPL to keep the BCCI happy, this meant another forced revision to the summer schedule.

The constant changes in the Covid protocols and rules in each state were only making it more difficult to confirm and lock a schedule. In September, the likelihood of Kohli's team starting their Test campaign at his favourite Test venue here, the Adelaide Oval, had gone up after the Western Australian state government declared that neither the Australian nor Indian cricketers will be shown any leniency in terms of quarantine regulations. This did lead to quite a bit of excitement in Adelaide, among local cricket fans and the local media. Some even dreamt of the possibility of a Boxing Day Test at the Adelaide Oval. Maybe even a New Year's Test to follow that.

South Australia's deputy chief public health officer Michael Cusack was quoted on the ABC website talking about the possibility of India being allowed to train in small groups. 'They will be allowed to train in what you might consider smaller bubbles. So, there might be three or four players that would be allowed to train during their quarantine period, and it would be the same consistent players.'

In the meantime, the BCCI had started to put some pressure on CA for the players' families to be granted permission to accompany them to Australia.[3] With thousands of Australians still stuck overseas, this was considered a step too high for CA to pull off. But they did let the Indians know that wherever they landed, a fourteen-day quarantine was mandatory by law.

---

[3] https://www.dailytelegraph.com.au/sport/cricket/aussie-summer-of-cricket-mcg-to-host-boxing-day-test-as-schedule-for-india-tour-released/news-story/79cbe2c82354500839343f40cda6ce0f

A senior player from the Test team, in fact, got in touch with us and told us that he was taking his wife to Dubai on a one-way ticket in the hope that she'd be allowed to accompany him with their daughter to Australia and that he would need some sort of confirmation from us to start looking at travel options for her.

The BCCI were adamant that it would work out only if their players were allowed to train during those two weeks. The ball was back in CA's court as they now looked around to find a state that would show some leniency.

On 15 October, Eddings was quoted in the *Australian* newspaper saying, 'I'm 100 per cent confident they are coming. Sourav Ganguly and I talk about it most days and we are already planning when we can catch up once he and the team get over here.' The report also stated that the players would land in Brisbane instead of Perth or Adelaide, and would not face much strictness in terms of quarantine time despite the state of Queensland seeing severe restrictions at that time.

Queensland had emerged as the first preference after the state had successfully staged the National Rugby League (NRL) and Australian Football League (AFL) competitions over the previous four months. A lot of the AFL and NRL teams were housed in plush resorts in south-east Queensland, and CA felt that a similar set-up would be arranged for Team India. Many believed, though, that the looming state elections in Queensland would end up determining whether this process would go through smoothly and without any late drama. As expected, reports began emerging that talks between the Queensland health department and CA had developed a hitch, even as Eddings and Ganguly continued to make 'catch-up plans'.

I had to chase the Queensland Health authorities for an update. 'Queensland Health is currently assessing an application received from the Indian cricket team. We will work directly with the team as the assessment progresses. We are unable to provide any further details while the assessment is still under way,' was the response I got.

Contingency plans were being discussed all around. The overall tour was worth A$300 million, with the white-ball leg of the trip expected to garner close to A$190 million. CA was desperate to ensure that, in the worst-case scenario, at least the T20Is and ODIs would take place.

As we continued to respond to queries from various members of the Indian team and support staff, the real question now was what their port of entry would be.

Western Australia had already slammed the door on returning international cricketers months ago, while the Adelaide Oval hotel, which had quarantined the Australian ODI team after they'd returned from the UK, had been ruled out—the South Australian government had deemed it unacceptable as an isolation facility. CA were slowly running out of options.

As of 15 October, the plan was for Australia and India to play six white-ball matches in south-east Queensland, before heading to Adelaide for the first Test. By 18 October, the Queensland solution was a no-go. The health authorities there had put their foot down, denying Indian players the permission to go out and train while in quarantine. This was an about-face that CA hadn't been prepared for. The walls seemed to be closing in on this seemingly ill-fated but highly lucrative and important Indian tour.

The state that had the most relaxed border rules throughout the first wave of the pandemic in Australia was New South Wales (NSW). On 22 October, Ben Horne, that champion of a news hound, broke the story in the *Daily Telegraph* that Sydney would host the tourists for the initial stage of the tour. Horne wrote, 'Cricket Australia is still awaiting a final sign-off on their schedule from the all-powerful BCCI, but sources said the NSW Government had given their approval for the Indians to quarantine and train in Sydney which is a major breakthrough in ensuring the $300 million summer gets off the ground.'

With NSW's government having thrown a lifeline—and it seemed more like they were sticking their hand out to pull CA ashore from a sinking boat—it was decided that the SCG would host four matches—two ODIs and two T20Is—while Canberra would get an ODI and a T20I each. Having saved CA from incurring a loss of A$300 million, it only seemed like a fair bargain.

The fixture was finally beginning to take shape, having gone through multiple modifications over the months leading up to this point. The only way the tour could now potentially be derailed was if the state government rejected the BCCI's request that the players' family members be allowed to travel to Australia. Considering most Indian players were looking at spending two months in Australia, on the back of an exhaustive eight-week, bubble-bound IPL, it only seemed a fair ask for them to want their partners and kids around.

There were some murmurs in Australian cricket circles that this was just the BCCI playing hardball, that common narrative which gets thrown around every time a national cricket board has to deal with the BCCI. With some sources even insisting that there had been no 'roadblocks' for family members of the Indian contingent to come over.

Finally, on 25 October, the tour schedule was all but confirmed between the countries, with the NSW government approving CA's strict biosecurity plans. But the messages and queries kept popping up on our phones. At least one member of the touring party was prepared to see the bright side of being in a bubble for the duration of the tour. His message read, 'Best tour then. Easiest tour to pack for. Even I can travel light this time.'

4

Hardik Comes of Age

'Aisa kya bol diya usne?'

It was perhaps the first time since we've known each other that I'd sensed genuine concern in Ravi Shastri's voice. The date was 8 January 2019, and we were at the lovely old bar at the InterContinental Sydney. Gaurav and I had received a phone call earlier that day from the head coach asking us to join him and Bharat Arun for a drink that evening. It was the day after Virat Kohli's team had become the first from India, and the Asian subcontinent for that matter, to win a Test series in Australia. There was still very much a celebratory air about the team hotel, and so too among the two key members of the coaching staff. We'd just about finished our second bottle of some fine South Australian red wine when Shastri's phone went off. He didn't bother looking at it the first time. But when it rang immediately afterwards, he had to. All we heard him say was, 'Oh, really? Oh, shit' a few times before looking at Arun and going, 'Boss, we have a busy night ahead of ourselves.'

The caller had just informed him about the mayhem back home over some controversial comments from Hardik Pandya on the TV show *Koffee with Karan*, where he had appeared alongside teammate K.L. Rahul. While Shastri knew that Hardik's candour on the show had caused a stir, he wasn't yet aware of the magnitude of the aftermath. It was then that he turned to us wondering if we'd seen the show, to find out the details of how Hardik had offended a great many with his words. Well, we had watched it, at least the clips that mattered, earlier that day. A few more volleys of 'oh, really?' and 'oh, shit' followed before Shastri and Arun excused themselves, apologizing for the earlier-than-planned finish to the night, and headed straight upstairs, looking for Hardik.

Ironically, the person who had directed our attention towards the show was none other than Hardik Pandya himself. It had happened the previous night, really late at night to be precise. The Indian team had, understandably, decided to let their hair down in every way possible after having achieved a feat that nobody else from their part of the world ever had. Gaurav and I were around in the lobby meeting a couple of our friends when we saw Hardik and Murali Vijay walk in through one of the many entrances of this plush hotel. While we exchanged pleasantries—it was good to bid adieu to Vijay in particular, who you kind of felt might not be a part of this team again—Hardik began plugging his appearance on the show. To be honest, he seemed genuinely oblivious to the storm that was brewing back home over his comments on the highly rated and popular talk show. Dressed in a rather extravagant pair of pyjamas, he insisted that we go and watch the episode, because 'the whole world was talking about it'. He wasn't wrong on that front. But clearly, nobody had told him yet what was actually being said about it all over India.

This is not to criticize or to defend Hardik and his comments. We are neither judge nor jury. I do believe, though, that people change, and people grow up. Everyone deserves a second or a third chance. There isn't anyone among us who hasn't regretted something they said in the past, or those who don't want to take back an opinion or a view that they shared in a public or private space. And in that moment, Hardik didn't come across as if he was being cocky about the whole affair.

He seemed very much aware of the consequences of what had transpired the next time we saw him, a couple of days later near the nets at the SCG. He had his head down, and the smile was gone.

Virat Kohli had been flooded with questions about the same issue earlier in the day. And he'd not held back in distancing his dressing room from the 'inappropriate comments'. The coaching staff let us know that Hardik and Rahul had been given a dressing-down in 'no uncertain terms'.

The customary hundred-odd fans who'd gathered around the SCG practice area were mostly kind to the duo, unlike the volley of jeers headed their way on social media. Still, Hardik and Rahul had quietly walked past them on their way back from the nets, ignoring their requests for selfies and autographs. Later that day, they were officially suspended with immediate effect, and an inquiry was ordered.

Such were the unceremonious and downright humiliating circumstances under which Hardik's previous tour, in 2018–19, to Australia had ended. So, when he returned to these shores nearly twenty months later, there was more than just the will to set the record straight. Though India's 2020–21 tour of Australia will forever be remembered for the feats of their Test team, the tone in some ways was set by Hardik and his exploits during the white-ball leg. A couple of months before Rahane & Co. pulled off the greatest heist in Test cricket history, Kohli & Co. had made quite a dramatic comeback themselves, recovering from two heavy defeats at the start of the ODI series to win the third one and the T20I series—thanks to Hardik Pandya and his coming of age.

Hardik has divided opinion like few have in Indian cricket ever since he broke on to the scene nearly a decade ago. While there has never been any doubt over his ability as a cricketer, his on-field performances, for the longest time, were judged in the light of how he carried himself off the field, even if this was a tad unfair. This perhaps had more to do with Indian cricket never having had someone quite like Hardik, who was prepared to not conform to this somewhat archaic idea of how an Indian cricketer should be. In pro-wrestling parlance, Indian cricket fans could never quite decide whether Hardik Pandya was a 'face' or a 'heel', a hero or a villain. They had a love–hate relationship with him even more than they'd had with Virat Kohli in his younger days.

And Hardik was aware of this. In an interview he gave me back in 2017, right before the Champions Trophy in England, the all-rounder spoke about wanting to evolve as a person: 'If people need to understand me, then I need to be more balanced, instead of only being the "I'll be myself" kind of guy.' There probably were also some harsh lessons learnt from the talk-show misadventure, not to forget the inherent maturity that comes from becoming a father. For, the Hardik we saw in November 2020 just seemed more well-rounded than ever before. There was a calmness about him. There was a sense of ease and control with who he was rather than who he was trying to be. And it began to show in his batting very early in the tour. The fact that he couldn't bowl much at all perhaps added to the amplified focus towards his batting.

Hardik ended up averaging 105, with a strike rate of 114.75 across the three ODIs. That included a valiant 90 off 76 balls as India failed to chase down 375 at the SCG, and a game-turning 92 off 76 balls to set up a victory in the third match at the Manuka Oval. What stood out about the knock, apart from the impact it seemed to have on the team's morale and on the eventual result, was the cerebral nature of it. It was a glimpse into Hardik's growth as a batter, both in terms of maturity and skill. His battles against Adam Zampa in particular during the limited-overs matches were right up there with the highly anticipated Kohli vs Cummins clash coming up in the Test.

It was mainly in his handling of the classy leg-spinner that Hardik began to really show his new-found ability to bat in different gears. The way he'd look to play out Zampa—rather than backing himself in an 'I'll be myself' fashion—and score runs off the other bowlers. The way he'd restrain himself even when the wily New South Welshman would try to lure him out of the crease. And the way he'd make up for it by relying on his greatest strength: his faultless power-hitting. It even prompted me to write a piece about how Hardik Pandya, the rockstar of Indian cricket, had 'learnt to take stock'. (It was a bad play on 'Michael Learns to Rock', and I realized over time that not many really got the dubious reference.)

Hardik's heroic finish at the SCG to seal the T20I series was the perfect culmination of his redemption on Australian soil: to come back and be hailed as the ultimate hero after having been dismissed as a classless villain. No wonder he held his pose for a while after smashing Daniel Sams for the second of the two sixes in the last over, making sure the match didn't go to the last delivery.

A brief exchange between Hardik and Shreyas Iyer at one point during their match-winning partnership that night serves to highlight the level of understanding that the Baroda big-hitter had acquired of his own abilities. At one stage in the match, Hardik felt like the target was rapidly getting out of reach. The team needed 37 off three overs. Hardik had struggled to get Zampa away, and frustration was setting in. Iyer had observed that Hardik was getting agitated. So he walked up to him and said, 'Don't worry about Zampa. I will take him on. You stay till the end.'

Duly, Iyer smashed the next ball for a six and finished the over with a boundary. That was all Hardik wanted. At the end of that over, it was Hardik who walked up to Iyer and, with a very satisfied smile, said, '*Bass, abhi me dekh lunga* (Leave it to me now).'

That was exactly what he did. After the game, Hardik spoke about having broken the bat he'd been using for the previous three years and the fact that he needed to find a new one. And he did seem to end up with a very nice new piece of willow—on a tour in which India ended up with a very nice, new Hardik Pandya.

★ ★ ★

It wasn't only with his batting that Hardik stood out during the first half of India's tour. This was probably also when we saw the emergence of Hardik Pandya the leader. Even as far back as late 2020, not many were really looking at the wiry all-rounder as anything more than a joker in the pack, who, on his day, could produce head-turning performances to win matches for his team.

But from very early on in the ODI series—in fact, from the first fifteen minutes of play itself—you could see Hardik taking a very active role at mid-off. If he wasn't in the bowler's ear, he was helping them set their fields. He also seemed to be the in-between man working constantly with Kohli and the likes of Bumrah and others, helping them come up with plans. He was the first one to give the bowlers a pat on the back or put an arm over their shoulder, as with Navdeep Saini when he was struggling with his length. So much so that at times, Kohli didn't mind leaving some of his younger bowlers completely in Pandya's hands. And as we've seen him in the IPL leading the Gujarat Titans, Pandya's was never an overbearing presence on the field. He would offer only a quick word of advice or encouragement to the other players.

There was also that moment during the second ODI in Sydney when Hardik proved that he was ready to put his body on the line for his team, even if it meant risking his own future. He'd been picked for the tour mostly as a pure batter in the hope that he would slip in a few overs if needed. The team management had informed him, based on the information received from the strength and conditioning coach, that at most he could bowl two overs on the trot. That was to also be his maximum quota for a given day's play, regardless of the format.

India had struggled on the field in the first ODI. Their bowlers had looked a tad rusty, and Kohli had struggled to find ways to plug the run flow, especially against Steve Smith. There had actually been an impromptu audition for the role of the sixth bowler an hour before the second ODI was to start. Mayank Agarwal was the one who got the nod. Not the most promising of signs for a team trying to shake off a heavy defeat.

Much like in the first ODI, the bowling continued to be wayward, with Mohammed Shami and Navdeep Saini creating no pressure and going at nearly 10 runs an over. Bumrah was having an off day too, which was confirmed when he, with great angst and frustration, kicked at a couple of thirty-yard fielding markers, which went flying a long way.

Still desperately looking for options and having given Agarwal an over already, Kohli was left with no choice but to turn to his wild card. With the dressing room looking on nervously, on came Hardik, running in at full tilt. He didn't look to be in too much discomfort either. His first two overs were not only on target, they also put the brakes briefly on the Australian onslaught for the first time in the series. Having come in on the back of a flurry of boundaries scored off the other bowlers, he didn't concede even one in those two overs. That was to be the end of his spell. But Hardik didn't think so.

His team needed him, and he was going to answer the call even if he knew he shouldn't. He nearly stormed towards Kohli and grabbed the ball from him for a third over, in which he got rid of Steve Smith, who'd scored his second 60-ball century in three days. At the end of that over, he waved off the physio, who'd come running in, and stuck a hand up to the dressing room, as if to say he was in charge of his own body now. For good measure, Hardik ran in for a fourth over too and should have had Marnus Labuschagne's wicket as well, but for a very rare dropped catch by Ravindra Jadeja. Hardik's spell did slow the Aussies down a bit but couldn't stop them from raking up their highest ODI total against India at that stage. It also meant that Hardik was too sore to bowl in the next match or in the subsequent T20Is. Nobody was complaining, though, not after he'd answered his call of duty so courageously.

With Virat Kohli scheduled to leave after the first Test, I did wonder whether Hardik would be kept back as a pure batting option for the Test series. There was the incredible form he was in, of course. But there was also his ability to lift his teammates and stick by them, as we'd seen during the hectic white-ball segment of the tour.

I did even cheekily suggest to one of the senior coaches that it might not be a bad idea to keep him back for the Tests, since some of the reserve bowlers were anyway being made to stay. I was told that it was 'a damn good idea' and that it would be considered. It wasn't to be, and I'm not sure whether it was considered at all. Not that I imagined they needed my 'expert' opinion to do so anyway.

Incidentally, the coaching staff had been very keen on potentially bringing Hardik in for the World Test Championship final, even if it was on a one-match basis. Gaurav and I had been told this earlier that year, when we were in New Zealand for India's tour. There was a feeling that Hardik could be quite the boost to India's arsenal at Lord's (which was where that match was originally scheduled to be held) for a Test in May, even if it meant wrapping him in cotton wool, as far as his bowling went, for a whole year. That idea did get shelved at some point. The rise and rise of Jadeja as one of the finest all-rounders in world cricket might have had something to do with it too, in addition to the uncertainty about Hardik's ability to bowl a decently long spell.

Hardik would have loved being there. To be a part of the showcase spectacle, yes. But more so because he's always wanted to play Test cricket. And for all his 'I'll be myself' approach in the early days, there were times he was understandably eager to know how he was perceived by the higher-ups in Indian cricket, starting with the national selectors.

Gaurav recalls the time when he was doing some commentary work for India A's tour of Australia in September 2016. This was when Hardik was very keen on impressing upon the selectors that he shouldn't be typecast as a white-ball specialist due to his eye-catching IPL exploits, and that he should also be considered for the longer format. Hardik had made quite an impression, as expected, during the one-day leg of the tour, winning the Player of the Match award on a couple of occasions. He'd been interviewed at the time by Gaurav for the Cricket Australia website.

Hardik had also noticed my intrepid colleague chatting away to one of the national selectors on tour quite often. After a few random run-ins, he decided to pick Gaurav's brains to see if there was any input at all he could gather about his own prospects. 'They know you're cut out for the limited-overs matches but still have doubts if you can perform as a batter in the longer format of the game,' Gaurav told him.

Hardik wasn't convinced with this view and pushed his case citing the number of Ranji Trophy matches he'd played for Baroda and also the number of times he'd bowled 15–20 overs in an innings. Gaurav, clearly sinking his teeth further into this unexpected role of being the conduit between the selectors and a potential star, let Hardik know that he would still have to score runs in tough conditions and situations to strengthen his case.

As it turned out, in the next four-day match at the Allan Border Field in Brisbane, Hardik made 79 off 116 balls, having come in to bat with the score at a precarious 46/6 against a very seasoned attack of Chadd Sayers, Kane Richardson and Jackson Bird. He also bowled 18 overs in Australia A's only innings for good measure.

Gaurav would bump into Hardik near the boundary ropes later during that game. Hardik had a smile on his face and a polite question for Gaurav: '*Abhi kya bol rahe hain* (What are they saying now)?'

Two months later, Hardik Pandya made his debut for India in ODIs. A year later he was playing Test cricket for his country. Six years later, he was leading a brand-new franchise to IPL glory in their first season, before getting a taste of captaining his country.

In that 2017 interview, he'd also talked about his journey towards self-discovery, which he'd embarked upon in recent years. It involved his going for long walks to 'think about life'. His brief yet impactful stay in Australia this time around had allowed us the chance to discover a lot more about Hardik. More so about aspects of him that we can like and admire. The turnaround was complete.

★ ★ ★

There was no shortage of drama during the white-ball part of the tour. But it would have paled in comparison to what was to follow. There was hardly a day when we were allowed to simply go through the motions in Australia. To start with, the unpredictable weather kept the players, and everyone else, on their toes. The first two ODIs in Sydney were played at a time when the city was engulfed by a heatwave so bad that we would see water helicopters constantly hovering over the drier suburbs, especially in the west, close to Gaurav's home. It meant a lot of fluid consumption, a lot of sweaty arms and a lot of players left completely drained by the sultry air.

By the time we returned from the Canberra leg a week later, Sydney had been hit by a cold wave from the western part of the country, resulting in the players now walking out in jumpers and some even carrying handwarmers in their pockets. Australia, you freakin' beauty, as they say.

One vital member of the Aussie camp, who couldn't make it to Canberra, was David Warner. He'd suffered a rather painful injury while trying to field a ball at mid-off during the second ODI at the SCG. So extreme was the opener's reaction that Justin Langer would later describe it so: 'It looked like he got shot by a gun.' Warner did hit the ground in a melodramatic fashion. But he had good reason to do that, having strained the abductor muscles in his groin, which, according to the majority of athletes, counts among the most painful of injuries. Warner continued to be in excruciating pain in the changing rooms after having somehow hobbled off the field. His wife, Candice, would joke the next day on local radio about not having been responsible in any way for having hampered Warner's groin, despite the fact that they had been 'reunited after four months apart'.

It was no laughing matter for the Australian selectors, though. Not only was Warner ruled out for the rest of the limited-overs matches, but the long recovery period needed for such a strain meant that it was very unlikely that he would be a part of the initial stage of the Test series. It was an early blow to the home team and, in a strange way, to India's mission of repeating their success from two years earlier, but this time with both Smith and Warner in the Aussie team.

T. Natarajan was having a much better week in Sydney. A couple of days before he'd made a somewhat unexpected international debut, the affable fast bowler from Tamil Nadu had accompanied fielding coach R. Sridhar and Washington Sundar to the popular Murugan temple in Westmead, only to be mobbed the most, within the social-distancing norms to an extent, for photos and selfies. All this before even getting his maiden India cap. Natarajan didn't mind the attention either, as seen in some of his social media posts from that time. Some others, like K.L. Rahul, preferred the solitude of the empty streets of Canberra— from 'solo riding' on an electric scooter to simply soaking in the silence around the peaceful suburbs.

The drive to Canberra is rather pleasant, especially when you can sit back and take in the English-style countryside in that part of Australia. The rolling hills and vast expanses of green, with a few old-school houses sticking their heads out in the distance. We did a stopover but went off the beaten track by avoiding Bowral, home of the Don's shrine, which attracts hundreds of cricket fans and journalists every year. We decided to stop next to the railway track in the tiny village of Wingello, home to the legendary Bill O'Reilly, who, let's say, would have backed our decision to skip Bowral and halt where we did.

Gaurav and I also managed to sneak in another little road trip on the off day following the third ODI. This time we went north to the cherry capital of Australia, the town of Young. Our main intention in going there was cricket-oriented. With Nathan Lyon's 100th Test coming up later in the summer, we thought this would be an ideal time to visit his hometown, where his parents still reside. We ended up at the Young Hotel and heard some lovely anecdotes from Garry and Marie Cummins, who run the establishment, about Lyon's exploits for the team that represented them in the local competitions. 'Dragon killer' was how Australia's most successful off-spinner had signed off at some point during the late 1990s on the notice board that the hotel still retains. There were other stories concerning how grounded he was, especially when it came to maintaining his connection with his roots. We were told that he often visited Young and was always most eager to help out with any event involving kids.

The Cummins were also keen on giving us an actual taste of Young's other famous export: their incredibly tasty cherries. We were whisked off by their son to his own orchard, some fifteen minutes away. There we got a tour of the rather expansive plot, along with a crash course on the various types of cherries. I can't, of course, tell you much about the intricate differences, but I can tell you that they each tasted as delectable as the next. We even got a discount on our cherry purchases that afternoon. I just picked the ones that looked the reddest.

Our evening plan that day also had a red theme to it, though this came to us in a bottle. It was our first meeting with Ravi Shastri and Bharat Arun for the tour. And despite the result of the ODIs not having gone their way, the two seemed in quite a buoyant mood. Maybe it was just the effect of seeing us. Or so we'd like to believe. But in all likelihood, it was the fact that they were allowed to be a little more out and about in Canberra, given that their hotel was equipped with a lovely outdoor dining area.

Our conversation, as always, covered a variety of topics ranging from the issues with the then New South Wales Premier, the impact of Covid on the trade of wine between South Australia and China, and their having to deal with being in a bubble—these were, don't forget, still early days of cricket in the pandemic era.

The focus eventually shifted to the slightly disappointing results in the fifty-over matches, Hardik's form with the bat, Kohli's departure after the Adelaide Test and how they were preparing for their defence of the Border–Gavaskar Trophy. There seemed to be an overall 'we have nothing to lose or to prove' vibe about their approach.

'We don't have Ishant [Sharma] or Rohit [Sharma]. Virat is leaving after one Test. We've told the boys to take this as an opportunity to grow. Even if we win one Test, that's a big victory. We've beaten Australia across all formats in their own den over the last few years. What do we have left to prove? So our focus is going to be centred on the younger players, and to see how they develop and mature in this cauldron of playing Australia in Australia,' we were told.

A day later, Justin Langer was seeing a lot of red too, this time at the Manuka Oval. The object of his ire was former teammate David Boon. Australia's head coach had stormed out of the dressing room and spent the innings break during the first T20I angrily gesticulating while making his displeasure known to the match referee. The issue was over India being allowed to use Yuzvendra Chahal as a concussion substitute for Ravindra Jadeja.

The Indian all-rounder was in the middle of an explosive innings when he injured his hamstring quite severely in the penultimate over of the innings. He decided to keep batting, though. He then received what, to start with, looked like a glancing blow to the helmet from Mitchell Starc off the second ball in the last over. Jadeja did not receive any immediate medical attention or a mandatory concussion test and batted on, smashing 9 runs off the last 4 balls, eventually finishing unbeaten on 44 off 23 balls.

Sometime during the innings break, it was learnt that Jadeja had started feeling dizzy and groggy, which confirmed that he had been concussed. That led to a confrontation between Langer and Boon, since Chahal the leggie had been accepted as a 'like-for-like' replacement. Australia felt that India were being given the unfair advantage of having the best of both worlds. It didn't help that Chahal played a huge role in India's win, taking three wickets, including Aaron Finch and Steve Smith, to end up as the player of the match. While Finch and Moises Henriques, who faced up to the media that night, decided to play down the issue, Langer's reactions were very suggestive of how the swap was perceived in the Australian dressing room.

Now, according to those in the Indian camp, the sequence of events went something like this. Sanju Samson, who had been dismissed earlier, was the first one to see it happen. He immediately informed Mayank Agarwal, who was seated next to him, that the blow was flush on Jadeja's helmet. Agarwal then ran up to inform the team management, by which time the game had moved on. Jadeja was met by two of the senior management staff on his way to the dressing room and had complained about feeling 'disoriented'. He was taken away by the medical staff to have his neck and head iced, while the coaches approached the match referee with Chahal as their nominee for being the concussion substitute.

A day later, the Indian team management completely dismissed the allegations from some quarters about their having used the blow to Jadeja's head as a 'tactical move' to bring Chahal in, since they were aware that the all-rounder's hamstring was badly injured. I was told in no uncertain terms that the only thought behind replacing Jadeja was to do with his overall well-being, considering the knowledge we have these days about the dangers of head trauma. Even the gripe about the physio not having run out to check on Jadeja the moment he was struck on the helmet was said to be unsubstantiated. The ICC's protocols, after all, say that the player can be checked on at the end of the over, and since Jadeja was struck in the final over of the innings, that didn't even matter. Jadeja underwent an MRI test the next day and was thankfully found to be out of any serious danger. He was said to be in quite a bit of strife with his hamstring, though, rendering him very likely unfit for the first Test. But a senior team official I spoke to reiterated that they weren't thinking about his hamstring when they walked to Boon's room to ask for a substitute. 'It's quite ridiculous that someone would think we would use one of our batsmen getting hit on the head as a tactic for anything,' I later quoted him as saying.

The next day at the Drummoyne Oval, I was greeted by Ravi Shastri, who looked at me and shouted, '*Arey* what senior team official? You should have just bloody put my name there. Let them know how I felt about this nonsense,' before letting out a loud guffaw.

5

The Real Prep

'Stop the car and pull over. I have a different plan for Australia.'

It is July 2020. While sitting in his beach house in Alibaug and watching a few old matches, Ravi Shastri feels like he's identified a chink in Australia's armour. He picks up his phone and makes a call to Bharat Arun.

'I feel like we should be attacking more on the line of the stumps or more at the body than outside off stump. On previous occasions we have attacked [Steve] Smith outside off and most of their runs [Smith's and Marnus Labuschagne's] were on the off side. Maybe even as high as 70 per cent. Why don't we change the line of attack? Why don't you devise a strategy?' This was his rather direct message to his bowling coach.

At this point, not only was the Australian tour over four months away, but there were still plenty of doubt if India could actually travel to Australia in the Covid-stricken world. Despite all those uncertainties, Arun decided to explore Shastri's idea. The video analyst was roped in to gather all the data on scoring zones for Australian batters in the last few years.

'I checked with the analyst. He said 70–75 per cent of their runs were indeed through the off side, but that was also because most teams had bowled more on that fourth-stump line,' Arun tells us now.

Shastri and Arun discussed the strategy on a few occasions over the phone. One aspect they agreed on was that the Australian batters could be tied down if the right field placements were applied, just like New Zealand had done to them a few months earlier in Australia.

'We had concluded after watching a lot of footage that a lot of their batters weren't getting runs on the leg side, unless it was a short ball. Or via a nudge or off the inside edge of the bat. You basically don't have fields for those shots or inadvertent shots. There are no catchers, there is not much protection, so even from middle stump, if you are going to attack that line, then have a field with catchers on the leg side and prevent the singles,' he adds. The plan was taking shape now.

One aspect of the strategy the pair was confident about was that it would certainly stem the flow of runs. Having observed the Australian batters on the two previous tours, in addition to the video footage, the Indian think tank had concluded that it was unnatural for the Australian batters to force length balls through the leg side, like most Indian batters can. Unless the Indian bowlers erred in length by bowling too short, the plan could prove effective.

If the strategy was to be implemented, the first process was to ensure that the captain and vice-captain were on board. Before proposing the idea to Virat Kohli, the rest of the coaching staff was informed about the mode of attack. The fielding coach, R. Sridhar, had to chalk out all the possible field placements to go with it.

During the seven-day lockdown in Dubai, before departing for Australia, the coaching staff roped in Kohli and Rahane on a Zoom call to finalize the devised plan. It wasn't as dramatic as Douglas Jardine getting his troops together on board the ship to reveal his masterplan against Don Bradman. But you couldn't deny the similarities, even if this plan lacked the viciousness and violence of bodyline.

'First, Virat had to agree to it. Ajinkya was in the meeting as well, because he was the vice-captain, and he was likely to lead after the first Test. It was a thorough session, because we talked in great detail, including about the fields as well,' informs Arun.

After a lengthy discussion, it was agreed that they try it on an experimental basis. The rest of the group would be told about the plan once the team landed in Australia.

★ ★ ★

'There are venomous brown snakes out there! Be careful, they have warned us from day one about not going to retrieve any balls from outside the ground. Don't take the risk. Just ask and I will provide you with the details.' There was deep concern in Bharat Arun's voice. And he was clearly very worried about our well-being.

Understandably so. Gaurav and I had taken quite the risk earlier that afternoon to get a peek at India's training sessions at the Blacktown Oval. Thankfully, we did so without the knowledge of these killer snakes. That ignorance maybe helped us stay safe inadvertently.

The thing was that we had no other option but to put ourselves in harm's way to squeeze out some information about what India were trying to work on in preparation for the big series coming up.

The Blacktown Oval's remote location had as much to do with our travails. The main entrance was off a small road that led to a gate patrolled by security. With team India in a bubble, the entrance had been sealed and was even guarded by a police car. So the most obvious vantage point had been taken away from us. More than half of the facility was surrounded by high eucalyptus trees and long, unkempt grass—the perfect habitat for black and brown snakes in the summer. And the train track behind the ground, with large fences erected alongside, made it impossible to access it on foot from behind.

So the only way out for us was the 'bushwalk' that Gaurav had charted before my arrival in Sydney to this point in between the bushes and two of the Ovals being used by the Indian team for their practice.

If the possibility of our catching a sneak preview of their practice was hindered by all these obstructions, they'd also covered most of the ground with black sheets. Eventually, we realized that our best option was to crawl up the grassy slope, bear a few scratches to the knees and elbows, stick our necks under the black sheet and spot whatever we could from there. Also, the only way for us to avoid slipping down that slope and injuring ourselves further was balancing our prone bodies by resting most of our weight on some of the overgrown creepers propping up from underneath. In all this, we did manage to use our binoculars to zoom in to see what the batters and bowlers were up to.

It might sound like we were part of some major yet ill-equipped espionage operation. And it did feel like that for the couple of hours we were there before rain interrupted our mission. You may also wonder why it was so important for us to take all this effort to simply watch a bunch of cricketers go through their routines. It's not like we were there to watch a live match. But I've always compared myself watching practice sessions and the nets to a car enthusiast spending time watching a set of wheels being put together on in a workshop. It gives you so much more perspective and context when you actually see a player do what he or she does best in the middle. I'm sure this analogy works similarly when you're talking about a car's performance on the road.

But our foray through the bush was completely worth it for one moment, if for nothing else. It was the day Mohammad Siraj had come to practise for the first time after having lost his father and having decided to stay back for the tour rather than go home for the funeral. To see the team rally around him, and then to see him run in at full tilt and celebrate a wicket by pointing towards the heavens, will stay with us as some of the most iconic moments of the tour.

It was only much later during that tour, as India began turning the corner in the Test series, that we realized how significant those twelve days of training in Blacktown had been for them. This was their 'true preparation', and it covered all angles, from bonding and planning to training and executing. The players and the coaches would echo our thoughts too, eventually.

'We absolutely relished those twelve days. It was the part of the day when we were free. We could joke, train, laugh and just gel as a group. There were close to fifty of us, so it felt like a massive camp. It reminded me of junior camps, but this was with the most elite players in India. I don't think such a camp or training will ever happen again on a tour,' one of them recalls now. It also helped that the ground staff would get everything ready for the Indians and leave once they were here. It added to the private-camp feel of the training sessions.

It was all about shaking off the rustiness of being in a bubble and getting back into rhythm for the first couple of days, in addition to getting used to training under strict Covid protocols. Bottles of water were provided for the group but there would be no food on offer at the training for health-and-safety reasons.

'The first few sessions were all about fitness work and running. None of the guys had bowled more than four overs in a match. They were all coming from the IPL. Bumrah had bowled the most overs, and that was sixty-four overs. The trainers had to manage them. Forget Tests, they weren't even ready for ODI cricket,' one of the coaches would tell us.

As one of the physios put it, 'IPL was totally different, but before that, for nine months due to Covid, the guys had hardly bowled. Running on an actual pitch or the ground is totally different to running on a treadmill or on indoor surfaces. We had to prepare them almost from scratch.'

The coaches also had to come up with ingenious methods to plan for these sessions. Separate Zoom calls with batters and bowlers, followed by further plans being discussed on the bus or in Blacktown before training. Then came the splitting of the white-ball players and the Test specialists.

The IPL-returned Australian players were also using the same facilities for their training, but they were always scheduled to do so during the mornings. It meant that the Indians also had to acclimatize to the heat of the Sydney summer. 'It is hotter than Dubai. This is such dry heat, and after not getting any fresh air for 18–20 hours a day, it takes a bit of time to get used it. Don't forget, we generally trained only in the evening time in Dubai. Here we are in the middle of the day. But it is great, we will adapt quicker,' one of the players explained.

There was some consternation over the state of the pitches in Blacktown, with members from both camps lamenting about the pitches being too sticky and not fit for ideal preparation for a white-ball series.

The one key member of the support staff missing during this part of the tour was throwdown supremo Raghu, the man who Virat Kohli believes—and Kohli actually pulled me aside in Port of Spain once to give him a special mention—has helped Indian batters improve against fast bowling. Raghu had tested positive for Covid before leaving India and was made to self-isolate in a hotel. He would later emerge a couple of weeks later—having been made to quarantine for an additional week owing to a false-positive test— and tell us, '*Bhagwan kare kisiko nahi ho jo mujhe hua* (God willing, nobody has to suffer the way I had to over the last two weeks).'

Once the sessions moved to centre-wicket practice, the players across formats were made to practise match simulations, and the reserve bowlers, Kartik Tyagi and Ishan Porel, were made to put in the hard yards. It was also a great learning curve for them, bowling alongside Bumrah and Shami, and under the constant supervision of Bharat Arun, who treated them like they were part of the squad and not just here to bowl in the nets.

'Firstly, even the likes of Shami and Bumrah hadn't bowled long spells for a long time. Plus, it was a long tour, so we had to get the youngsters involved . . . After a few days, it was evident to us that the absence of net bowlers was going to lead to a heavier load on all the fast bowlers. Ravi decided to keep the likes of Tyagi and Natarajan, and even Shardul later, on for the entirety of the tour . . . It was important we treated them like they were regular members of the Test squad, even if it meant making them do the 2K time trial. It was all about unity. Maybe that's what allowed a couple of them to end up playing like they belonged, eventually,' Arun explained.

In fact, there was lack of clarity over whether the net bowlers would be provided at all for India through the tour. I remember getting this issue crosschecked with a CA staff member, who assured me that they were available. But when I passed the information on to the Indian coaching staff in Adelaide, they mulled it over and decided that they would manage with Natarajan, Tyagi and Shardul Thakur.

As one bowler recalled later, the focus for the fast bowlers who were part of the white-ball squads was more on workloads—it was about getting them to bowl 9–10 overs in the day in sessions that were split up with a lunch break in between.

'First, we had to get our limits from four overs to ten overs. The aim was to be able to bowl ten overs comfortably at the end of the fourteenth day,' says one of the fast bowlers who stayed back for the Tests.

The goal for the coaching staff was to get Kohli & Co. up to at least 60 per cent match intensity in preparation for the coming series before they left Blacktown.

While watching the session, Gaurav and I were struck by a left-hander who kept driving Bumrah and Shami on the rise through the covers. He also played swivel pull shots and seemed to be handling the pacers too easily. It was only on closer inspection that we discovered that the left-hander was Washington Sundar. This wouldn't be the only time he'd impress us with his batting.

The tasks handed out to the batters and bowlers were very specific. They ranged from getting the openers to get to 20 for no loss in ten overs, while having Pujara and Rahane get together with the virtual score at 20/3 in ten overs, and set them a target of 50/3 in twenty-five overs. For the bowlers it was all about getting rid of the openers within the first 6–7 overs. These goal-oriented sessions would last for two and a half hours each and, in many ways, set the blueprint for what was to come.

One development that caught our eye immediately was Hardik Pandya marking out his run-up. He had not bowled during IPL 2020, and there were a lot of question marks over his 'bowling fitness'. We would later learn that Arun had been working on his action, and that the alterations would allow the all-rounder to be more injury-free in the future and also help him go back to bowling 140 kph consistently. A couple of years on, we can say that it certainly worked out all right.

★ ★ ★

On 20 November, Mohammad Siraj lost his father. The tragic news had come through overnight, and what made it even more terrible was that none of his teammates or coaches could go to his room to even see how he was doing.

'We had got back from practice. We were in quarantine. That moment where none of us could see and console him told a lot about Siraj. When we lose a near and dear one, we want to be around people, but here he was in his own room. We can only imagine what he went through,' says Arun.

While the manager and doctor had sought special permission to be able to spend some time with the bereaved fast bowler in his room, it wasn't granted. Siraj did receive multiple calls and a lot of support from his teammates and coaching staff. Sridhar would even manage to organize some Hyderabadi biryani for the youngster— anything to try and lift his spirits.

And it was so good again to see him back among the boys, enjoying his cricket just like his father would have wanted him to. It was also touching to see that even during training one of the players was always next to him, in case he needed some emotional support and also to ensure that he was never left alone again.

'It is tragic what has happened, but rest assured, each and every one of us is with you. Sadly, you father is no more, but he is looking at you and knows you will make him proud on this tour. You are a brave man to stay here and such is destiny. You will play Test cricket and, God willing, take a five-wicket haul.' These were Ravi Shastri's words to Siraj at the end of his first session back with the team. And how prophetic those words would prove to be! Later, Shastri would tell us that he wasn't sure if the prediction about Siraj's debut was going to come true, but in the moment what the youngster needed was a cuddle of any kind. This was it. And it worked.

There was some truth to Shastri's statement too. The coaching staff had, after all, identified Siraj as being the prime candidate for their 'leg-side theory'.

* * *

The team management had also noticed something about one of their senior-most players, which they felt needed addressing. As Bharat Arun reveals now, 'R. Ashwin wasn't being himself completely during the first few days of training.' He was still heavily involved with the goings-on but just not his typical self. They wanted to convey to Ashwin that he had a big role to play on this tour as the primary spinner and a senior player, regardless of where they were playing.

Arun said: 'Ravi and I observed that he was being aloof, not sure what the reason was. Initially, we thought, let us give him a bit more time. The great thing about Ashwin the bowler is that he is never satisfied about what he does, he always wants to come out of the comfort zone.

'I told him, "Ashwin, you know enough now. You don't need to come out of the comfort zone. Just focus on what you know and what you have done. If you can get that absolute consistency in that, I think, you will do great."

'He is someone who needs some amount of caring, which will get the best out of him. In his own heart, he would have felt he has not done well overseas, and people are looking at that, so he needed to be given that little amount of confidence for him to believe he still had the potential to achieve success overseas. To his credit, he also agreed. And then you just have to see the kind of impact he had on the series.'

Buoyed after the chat, Ashwin would also tell Arun about being more prepared than ever before to combat his old nemesis Steve Smith. 'He said, "Sir, I've watched a lot of footage and have planned exactly how I want to bowl to Steve Smith on this tour." More so on this tour, I'm extremely confident of executing all these things,' Arun told me.

It was decided that the ninth day of training would be an inter-squad forty-over match. The lights at Blacktown enabled the fixture to be a day/night match. It would be India's longest day out since arriving in Australia. The match commenced at around 1.30 p.m., and Rahul was the one who stole the show early before Kohli took over. We'll talk a lot more about that knock a few chapters down the line.

* * *

As the public's attention shifted towards the white-ball leg of the tour, as proved by the sizeable crowds that attended those matches, the Test batters focused on their preparations for the four-Test series. While the majority of squad members travelled to Canberra for the ODIs and T20Is, Pujara, Rahane, Ashwin, Shaw, Vihari and Saha stayed back and practised at the SCG. Batting coach Vikram Rathour, throwdown specialist Raghu and a physio accompanied them all for four days of practice.

This was time for Rahane to apply his new backlift. Throughout his career up to that point, he had tapped his bat, but this time around he wanted to just hold it in the air. These three sessions allowed the Test specialists to fine-tune their trigger movements and other aspects of their batting.

India had taken a similar approach in the 2018–19 series, when the then batting coach, Sanjay Bangar, had worked with the batters on some very Australia-specific plans. We learnt through one of the players that the primary purpose of these sessions was to ensure that the batters were getting accustomed to playing the 'length' the Australia fast bowlers would bowl.

'We knew we had done well against their bowlers on the previous tours, so we didn't have to change our approach or technique too much. It was more about getting used to the bounce, knowing what shots to play and just being in the right mindset,' one of them told us.

There were two three-day matches scheduled ahead of the first Test, the first of which commenced on 6 December at the Drummoyne Oval in Sydney. The condensed schedule meant that this game clashed with the final two T20Is of that series. And the coaching staff remained split up. The Drummoyne Oval is a beautiful venue with massive grassbanks on one end and a quaint little pavilion at the other. We were seated in a makeshift press box, separated from the Indian dressing room by nothing but a thin white cloth acting as partition.

On the morning of the match, we had an early phone call from one of the senior coaches asking us to apprise them of the proceedings in the first hour of play. It's fair to say there was a sense of disappointment in their voice when we described the manner of the three early wickets. 'We have told the guys for the first hour, give nothing to them. Can't be getting out in that fashion flashing. We have a while before the Test. We will sort it out.'

Initially, the game was supposed to be broadcast on TV, but Fox Sports had changed their mind at the last minute. It meant the support staff had nowhere to watch it on, till we sorted them out with the streaming service carrying the game. We were informed that the coaches would visit Drummoyne on Day Two.

Bizarrely, no spectators were allowed inside the ground due to Covid restrictions. Luckily for the Sydneysiders, the transparent fencing guaranteed a view from outside the ground boundaries. A crowd of close to 8000, mostly of Indian origin, sat along the fence or even perched themselves on the high fig trees to watch the action.

'This is bloody ridiculous. Such a beautiful setting, a nice day and some of the best players in the world are in our suburb, but CA wants to lock down the grounds. No wonder cricket is not growing in this country like before,' an enraged spectator would say later. (I can assure you that this wasn't Gaurav pretending to be an enraged spectator, even if he was forced to watch the first day from near the fence, owing to a shortage of space in the press box.)

It was perhaps the best kind of preparation that India could have asked for. A spicy pitch, a very decent bowling attack led by James Pattinson and Michael Neser, who were in a team led by Travis Head, with Test skipper Tim Paine behind the stumps. Not to forget the prodigious talent of Will Pucovski and Cameron Green. For some of them, this match would act as a selection trial.

The proximity to the dressing room did make for some interesting conversations which we overheard, though it would be very unfair to publish any of those. At many points, I had to shush a boisterous Rishabh Pant as he kept trying to make fun of Raghu in the loudest voice possible. There was also a rather sweet moment as I sat on the balcony with a padded-up Rahane sitting only inches away. We looked at each other, and I told him, 'Can you imagine we have spent the last fifteen years doing this? You going out to bat, and me then writing about you batting in the middle?' After a brief moment of contemplation, he shook his head and went, '*Haan yaar*, how did all that time go so quickly?' Soon enough he was in the middle, making a century that, in some ways, was similar in form and nature to the slightly more significant one he would score later in the tour. And I was doing what I'd always done, write about Ajinkya batting in the middle.

Pujara looked his solid self, but his most important contribution during the day seemed to come later where he took Hanuma Vihari under his wing and walked all around the Oval chatting away with the graceful right-hander who'd been earmarked by some to fill in that No. 3 spot once Pujara was on his way.

At the end of the day, we had to scramble off from Drummoyne across town to the SCG for the second T20I, and therefore we could not stay behind and pick some of the key players' brains a little more.

Day Two at Drummoyne was all about Ashwin bowling in a cap and Umesh Yadav bowling his heart out. 'Strongy', as Umesh is referred to by most of the coaches, had put in a strong enough performance on what was his fourth tour down under, to ensure his spot as the third seamer for the opening Test.

It was a sign of things to come when fielding coach, R. Sridhar, had to don the whites and go field for a few overs. India only had eleven fit players at Drummoyne, with Pant having missed out due to a not-too-serious neck strain, as they put it. Even the physio Soham was decked in the team kit, in case he was needed. There was an outside chance that either Gaurav or I might have been called in, too, to do a Henry Blofeld, who had famously once come close to a shock Test call-up on a tour to India—he was a journalist and the England team had been ravaged with sickness and injury.

To Sridhar's credit, he didn't look even a bit out of place in the Indian jersey. Now we understood why he was so fussed about all the carbs he'd had with the pizza back in Canberra and what he was talking about when he said, 'I'll need to run all this off tomorrow.' He was understandably excited and nervous before going out to field. While he would have loved taking a catch to show that he'd still got it, there was also the worry of dropping a catch in front of the players and never being able to live it down as a fielding coach.

Just before lunch, a car carrying Shastri, Arun, Agarwal and Bumrah arrived at the ground. While the coaching staff talked to the senior members, every other member of the Indian team suddenly was on his feet, offering the head coaches chairs and bottles of water. Bumrah picked up a pair of shoes and headed to the nets situated behind the grandstand, where a bunch of brand-new pink Kookaburra balls were waiting for him. He then proceeded to bowl a very testing spell to Agarwal, who didn't have it easy.

'He wanted to get more bowling under his belt. The T20Is were only four overs, plus he wanted to practise executing the Test match lengths as well,' according to Arun.

Back in the middle, the afternoon session was all about Ashwin. With that cap still on, like he was Clarrie Grimmett, he would get the ball to dip, grip and turn with great control. The ball was beating both edges and asking innumerable questions of the batters, challenging their technique—especially after Prithvi Shaw finally managed to find a pair of loose trousers to fit his shin pads in and stand at short leg. With two wickets up his sleeve, Ashwin was greeted at the tea-break with many of his teammates walking over to him and patting him on the back. His spells here were reminiscent of the way he'd bowled in Adelaide in 2018 to set up that first Test win. And here he was displaying his prowess with overspin, and you could sense that he was primed for success on this tour. He could sense it too.

There were also some early signs of India's leg theory being deployed, with a leg gully and leg slip acting as fixtures for literally every Australia A batter who walked out for a hit. And as expected, the ball flew towards that area behind square.

Speaking of balls bouncing off surfaces, we spotted Prithvi Shaw and Shubman Gill involved in a lengthy chat about how difficult it was to force balls off the back foot, especially when away from the body, on these Australian pitches, and how they were used to getting away with it on the more placid pitches back home. Batting coach Rathour chanced upon this chat and chose to join in to appreciate their learnings from the Drummoyne Oval match.

The third day would also see the unfortunate blow to Pucovski's head off Tyagi's bowling just when he seemed primed to finally make that elusive Test debut. That it came very late in the day, and off a ball that didn't bounce as high as it could have, told you everything you needed to know about the young Victorian's horrid run of luck with head injuries. There was concern all around, and Rahane immediately headed towards the Australia A dressing room after the close of play to check on Pucovski. He then walked across, picked up all the stray bottles of water and chucked them in the bin, and asked us to keep him posted on the young opener's condition.

India might not have found too many performers of note in their first warm-up game, but there was plenty to learn from as references for the tougher challenges ahead.

'It was a superb pitch, like a typical Australian pitch. I have come here on a numerous occasions, but this was the best pitch we have got for a practice match. Also, their attack was so good. Normally in a tour match, the opposition bowlers can be below first-class level, but this was as good as a Test bowling attack,' one of the senior players would say.

In the meantime, there was confirmation Rohit Sharma had been ruled out for the first two Test matches, while Ishant Sharma had been deemed unfit for the whole series. We were informed by the team management that Rohit was at the National Cricket Academy and, once he proved his fitness, would be on his way to Australia. We had to inquire with CA about how Rohit would be able to enter Australia. It turned out that Rohit was going to be granted permission, since his name was on the initial list provided by the BCCI. However, if Rohit or any other player arrived from India, they would still have to endure the thirteen days of quarantine.

Two days later, the whole squad assembled at the SCG for the second tour match. There was some talk of Shreyas Iyer being added to the Test squad. But the day after the third T20I, news came through that Iyer was heading home. So, too, were Yuzvendra Chahal, Shikhar Dhawan, Deepak Chahar, Manish Pandey, Sanju Samson and Iyer.

The second tour match was supposed to be the proper warm-up game for the pink-ball Test, but against a relatively weaker bowling attack. It meant that India could focus on getting their Test match seamers game-ready. And Bumrah and Shami were right in the mix, enjoying some reasonably lengthy spells.

'It was not only about the overs they bowled, but the amount of time spent on the field. A bowler can deliver 30–40 balls in the nets, but after that he can rest. In the match you need to stand and field the ball. So, conditioning a bowler for a Test match is not simply about how many overs he has bowled,' one of the coaches explained.

Jadeja's injury meant Ashwin would be a certain starter at Adelaide. There was still a conjecture over the six batters and the opening slot, although we were adamant Shaw would be opening with Agarwal.

The diminutive Mumbai opener started off in grand style, smashing 40 off just 29 balls before getting out. We would bump into him in the nets later that day, and he'd say this to us with a kind of matter-of-fact boldness that we have come to love about Shaw: 'If I had stayed there till lunch, it would have been two hundred-plus.'

'The total score?' I asked him.

'No, no, my score,' he said.

He also gave the nod to Cameron Green, calling him the most challenging bowler he'd faced on tour and said that Green would be a certain starter come the first Test. He was right about that too, like he is with a lot of things, even if he's still figuring out his right tempo in Test cricket.

'One thing with Prithvi is that he can give you that fast start. Before you know it, the score is 70–80. Shot selection is key for him, he has all the ability. He cannot play forcing shots off the back foot during the initial few overs, though,' we'd hear from a member of the coaching staff.

It was also evident that the colour of the ball wasn't going to determine whether India would use their leg theory during the

Tests. We saw a few illustrations of that with the leg gully and leg slip being employed for both Shami and Bumrah.

On the field, Vihari went on to score an impressive century in the second innings. That was before Rishabh Pant stole the headlines, the first of many times on the tour, with a blazing ton, which was watched by a very decent crowd around the SCG. And you could see, as always, the man most excited by Pant's exploits was captain Kohli, who'd opted out of playing here. And you could see that his focus had already shifted to Adelaide. King Kohli was on his way.

6

'King' Kohli Sets the Stage

On 27 August 2020, Virat Kohli announced through social media that he was going to become a father soon. The news was received with understandable delight all around the cricketing world. It did lead to some anxiety in the corridors of Australian cricket, though. Not that you had anyone there who wasn't chuffed for Kohli. It was more to do with the impact this could potentially have on the Indian tour, in terms of the captain's availability.

Would Kohli come only for the white-ball leg of the tour? Would he miss the entirety of the Test series or only a part of it? Would he come at all?

The overall uncertainty over the protocols across the different states of Australia, and the nature of the bubbles that the teams would have to stay in, added to the speculation. With only a few weeks to go before India's scheduled arrival, there was another rather unexpected question doing the rounds in Australian cricket media circles: Where was Anushka Sharma planning to deliver her baby?

Both Gaurav and I had to convince some of our colleagues that she would not be making the trip under any circumstances. On one occasion, I had to explain the Indian custom of women travelling to their parents' homes for the delivery. I doubt I did a great job of breaking it down for my fellow journalist. It's not generally my area of expertise. But he got the gist of it. Or I think he did. He never asked me again.

'Wouldn't it make sense for her to come here and have the baby in Australia? We are among the best countries in the world when it comes to medical care. Plus, that'll mean Virat can stay till the end of the series,' another quipped semi-seriously.

Then, on 9 November, to everyone's relief, it became official. Virat Kohli would be on his way to Australia—sans his pregnant wife, as expected—and stick around till the end of the first Test in Adelaide. That gave the broadcasters enough time and scope to use the high-profile Indian captain as the fulcrum of their promotions for the high-profile Indian tour. That meant Kohli was everywhere. Including in some headlines, especially in the *Advertiser*, Adelaide's daily newspaper, in some hyperbolic proportions, ranging from 'Special One' to 'Adelaide Get Kohli to Themselves'. Another newspaper even designated what they called the 'Virat Kohli Week' to welcome him to Australia.

In fact, images of Kohli had started popping up on Australian television screens a few months before the tour was even officially confirmed. You'd turn on the six o'clock news on Channel 7 in Adelaide, only to see old clips of Kohli raising his bat following that famous century at the Melbourne Cricket Ground (MCG) in 2014. The sports headlines in the lead-up to the cricketing season seemed to be focused more on whether Australians would get to see 'King Kohli' on their shores come the summer. It felt as if the Indian team getting here was only incidental. I'm very sure I saw more glimpses of Kohli on Australian television and in newspapers during the whole of October 2020 than I ever did during any month-long period while living in India.

All eyes were, not surprisingly, trained on Kohli from the moment the Indian team arrived in Sydney, decked in black, like they were a bunch of stormtroopers from a *Star Wars* set. And Kohli remained in focus pretty much till the time he exited the Adelaide Oval on that dramatic December evening a month later.

Having that clarity around his involvement from even before the Indians departed for Australia was good for the rest of the

team too. It allowed them to plan and rally around each other a
lot better, right from the beginning. It was the same for the team
management. And Ravi Shastri made sure to address the team
about the unprecedented scenario of the captain leaving this early
on a tour.

Shastri is learnt to have said to those around him: 'Virat will
be going home, and I'm glad he made that decision up front. He is
doing the right thing, and I told him, ignore all the noise from back
home. This series is about youngsters, we will nurture a few heroes
on this tour. I've told the guys I know what Australia is about, and
they will try to mess with you from all directions, including the
media, but just be yourself, I will handle all that noise.'

The head coach also had a few words of advice for Gaurav and
me, which he reiterated on several occasions, during the early part
of the tour. 'Watch the captain,' he'd say pretty much every time
we bumped into him. And so we did watch the captain. What
caught our eye immediately were Kohli's intensity levels during the
white-ball matches of the series. It's not that he was taking it easy
or wasn't fully invested in the ODIs or the T20Is that followed; it
was more like he was conserving, maybe even saving up, some of
that inimitable feistiness for the one Test he was staying back for.
You could see this more in Virat Kohli the batter than Virat Kohli
the captain.

As leader, he was as animated and was, as usual, a part of every
moment of everything that transpired on the field, right from the
first time he had to captain the team on the tour: during India's
opening intra-squad match at Blacktown Oval during their first two
weeks of training within quarantine. When he wasn't scrambling
around his fielders to keep up with K.L. Rahul's assault, he was
giving Mayank Agarwal a polite send-off, especially once the
opener decided to stand his ground and debate his LBW dismissal
with 'umpire' R. Sridhar.

Kohli then sat in the dressing room, like he was hoping to find a
scenario that would get him into that special zone. He wouldn't be

the first great sportsperson, after all, to need some external stimuli to get going during a practice game, with nothing much at stake.

Thankfully for Kohli, his team found themselves in a rather tricky position when he walked out to bat, chasing a sizeable target in their forty overs. The onus was on him to now see his team home. Basically, the ideal set-up for a Kohli special. And he did turn it on, smashing 91 off 58 balls, on an up-and-down pitch that had many of the other batters, except Rahul, in trouble.

Kohli was certainly his boisterous self once the first ODI kicked off at the SCG. Being able to finally play in front of crowds again, for the first time in nearly ten months, was incentive enough. Not to forget the fact that this was Australia that he was up against.

It wasn't an afternoon to remember for Kohli and his team, as Australia piled on what was then their second highest ODI total against India. It wasn't so much the runs that were being leaked as the captain's lack of control over the proceedings that seemed to be bothering him. It was classic Kohli, frantically waving his hands and gesticulating at his fielders and bowlers. Occasionally throwing his hands up in despair or kicking the ground in disgust. His reactions seemed to get even more exasperated as his ragged teammates struggled to keep up with the heat in Sydney. Eventually, after many displays of displeasure, Kohli himself let a ball through his legs in the forty-ninth over of the Australian innings. This time he had no one else to stare at angrily.

Kohli's knock in the run-chase proved to be symptomatic of the team's rustiness, having just stepped out of their bubble. It came as part of a breezy and eventful passage of play. He was dropped early on at fine leg by Adam Zampa and followed it up with three breathtaking strokes—a pick-up shot, inside-out, over the covers, a brutal pull and a whip over mid-wicket that flew for six. Then a soft dismissal as he charged down the wicket to Josh Hazlewood and pulled him straight to Aaron Finch at mid-wicket inside the circle.

There was no drop in intensity of any kind when it came to the hype around him in Australia, though. The broadcasters weren't going to let slip even a single opportunity to milk the presence of the most popular cricketer in the world.

You'd see 'When we return, it'll be time for King Kohli', or 'King Kohli to the middle after the break' flash up as tickers at the end of the Australian innings and prior to India commencing their chase. Once again, the other ten who were scheduled to walk out to bat were simply incidental to the context of the match.

There was a bit more of vintage Kohli in the second ODI as he seemed to get India on track for the massive run-chase before getting out in pretty much the same fashion as he had two days earlier.

It was not until two weeks later, when he was back in the SCG nets, that Virat Kohli really seemed to have powered up fully. He'd entered that mode so unique to him, where every fibre of his being seems to have developed this single-minded determination to own the stage in front of him. Two years earlier, it was in Adelaide that Kohli & Co. kicked off their campaign successfully before eventually becoming the first Indian team to win a Test series in Australia. And the Indian captain looked very keen on making sure that he'd set up their Border–Gavaskar Trophy defence in a similar fashion before leaving Adelaide this time around.

There was some conjecture around Kohli deciding to play in India's only pink-ball warm-up game in Sydney. So much so that nearly every media organization had a representative on 'Kohli watch' in the SCG press box on the afternoon of 11 December. But to their dismay, shock even, it became rather obvious that he wasn't going to play. The broadcasters, who'd assembled a full-fledged commentary team, were also a touch disappointed as it reduced Kohli time further on TV.

Instead, while the rest of the Test players began warming up for the game, Kohli was seen running laps around the ground by himself.

Half an hour into the start of play, he was heading towards the practice area for a hit. Interestingly, it wasn't so much in terms of his own batting that you could make out how switched-on Kohli was; it came through a lot more from the batting crash course that he was providing to Mayank Agarwal.

The session lasted nearly thirty-five minutes. And throughout that period, Kohli's focus was completely on his opening batter. Agarwal had walked in straight after having been nicked off cheaply by Sean Abbott in the middle. Kohli didn't even wait to take his pads off before walking over to the Karnataka right-hander.

Agarwal had poked at a length delivery that rose to around chest height from Abbott and edged it to Joe Burns at first slip. He'd got into an awkward position while doing so, much like his struggles against Jasprit Bumrah at the Drummoyne Oval nets a few days earlier.

Agarwal wasn't the first overseas batter to be sorted out by the mythical extra bounce off an Australian pitch. Kohli had seen a few of his own teammates fall prey to it on previous tours, even if he'd himself always thrived on it in Australia. It only made sense, then, that Agarwal was all ears as Kohli turned temporary batting coach and mentor.

'Look, you did it perfectly the last few balls without thinking,' Kohli was overheard telling him at one point. He nearly sounded like a proud parent. He was beaming like one for sure.

The session commenced with a demonstration from Kohli on how Agarwal would be better off getting his hands higher while trying to shoulder arms to deliveries with extra bounce. The rationale behind it was to eliminate any chance of being pulled into a late prod, as is the case with a lot of overseas top-order batters, who are used to playing with low hands in their own conditions. In addition, Kohli suggested that it would also automatically help him finish up in a more front-on position, further dragging him away from the line of the ball.

Following that initial ten-minute lesson, Kohli walked over to the farthest net—two away from where Agarwal was—to observe from side-on not just where Agarwal's hands were but also what his feet were up to. India's throwdown specialists then began peppering Agarwal with short-of-length deliveries around where the fifth or sixth stump would have been.

Within a few deliveries, Kohli had noticed a discrepancy. 'Feel the back toe is raised,' he said to Agarwal, indicating that the right-hander's back leg was either in the air or in motion as he defended the specifically targeted deliveries. It was this error that had let him down an hour earlier against Abbott. In addition to his not being fully balanced at the crease, Agarwal was also naturally feeling for the ball with his hands, which was resulting in the edge.

Kohli's suggestion seemed to be based more around getting Agarwal to focus on a firmer front-foot press as a trigger movement—getting into the old boxer's stance, as the late Dean Jones loved referring to it. That would result in the batter being in a stronger position to go either forward or back, depending on the length of the delivery. It would also make sure that the back toe doesn't get raised. There were further demonstrations before Kohli suggested to Agarwal that he'd throw a few balls at him just to see if the adjustment could work out for him.

Kohli even stood behind the stumps at the bowler's end as the throwdown specialists continued to chuck down troublesome deliveries at Agarwal. And more demonstrations. At one point, Kohli tried getting Agarwal to stay a bit squarer to make sure that both his eyes were facing the bowler, giving him a clearer view of the ball from the time it was released to when it landed on the pitch.

It wasn't all technical. There were constant words of praise and commendation every time Kohli felt like his senior opener was being successful with this slight modification. He even began to look satisfied when, after eight or nine throwdowns, Agarwal's alignment seemed to align with his views. So involved was Kohli with his opener that he offered to stay back and keep throwing balls till the time he was content. 'You want some more. I can keep doing this,' you could hear him say a couple of times.

He continued chatting away with Agarwal, and so engrossed was he that R. Ashwin had to call out twice to get Kohli to move away from the net so that the off-spinner could commence his own batting stint. He waited for a few minutes after Agarwal left to walk back towards the dressing room.

It worked out well for me. For, it gave me the opportunity to not only catch up with Kohli after quite a few years but also clarify some of my takeaways from his coaching clinic. He started off by insisting that he would never ask a batter to try and change their technique during a tour or so close to the start of a series. It was about minor alterations. What he'd tried to work on with Agarwal was more to do with the mindset, in terms of being positive not just in the head but also with your footwork. It was about the transfer of weight and also how, in Australia, Kohli preferred his weight to be constantly pushing towards the ball. He spoke about how he wanted the head to stay still but the left shoulder to be leaning forward. This was to ensure that the batter was in a better position to meet the ball on the top of the bounce, and also in a better position to judge what deliveries should be left alone. His eagerness to get to the Adelaide Oval was palpable during the ten or so minutes we stood chatting.

Like Pujara, Kohli had opted to get acclimatized with the pink ball, which he had faced only once previously during a Test match, in the nets, rather than take on the likes of Harry Conway, Will Sutherland and Sean Abbott. He had quite the audience at the nets too. All four of the senior coaches had accompanied him, with the batting coach, Vikram Rathour, taking charge of the session while Ravi Shastri and Bharat Arun stood behind the net. Kohli's first point of interest was to do with his head position, and he asked the batting coach to let him know if his head fell away even once.

Here, too—as with Agarwal a little later—Kohli wasn't concerned only with his own game and was constantly in the ears of those bowling at him. There was a lot of praise for T. Natarajan, who twice beat Kohli's outside edge and also smashed into his pads with a skiddy delivery. Kohli did, at one point, ask him to change his length when the left-armer bowled three on the trot that were a bit too short for his liking.

Meanwhile, Kohli wasn't keen on Kuldeep Yadav's line and length, and felt that the left-arm wrist spinner could try and bowl a little quicker through the air. He also took time out to explain to Washington Sundar—who had been held back for the sole purpose of replicating the Nathan Lyon challenge in the nets—the benefits of pitching the off-break closer to off-stump. The goal was to enable him to create opportunities and get the ball to turn through the gap between the right-hander's bat and pad.

The most fun Kohli had was during his tussle against Shardul Thakur, even pulling him up in jest for having failed to camouflage a slower delivery on his pads well enough—a ball that he flicked away with timing and menace.

The following day was all about Kohli and Pujara, the engine room of the Indian batting line-up, finding their rhythm. Kohli went out first, kicking off his session with some knocking. He faced two sets of ten balls each from fielding coach R. Sridhar with a sidearm (or dog-thrower or wanger, as they are referred to in different parts of the world). The first of those was a bunch of full-length deliveries that he either defended or drove off the front foot.

He then wanted to play some shots off the back foot. It was then time for Kohli to get the grips sorted on a couple of his bats. In the adjoining net, Rathour and Sundar were busy scuffing up the pitch and creating a 'rough' zone for the key batters to practise on later. In an attempt to further zero-in on the spot, Rathour placed a stump a few inches from the net—where, say, a seventh stump would be—and did so at a similar spot at the bowler's end too.

Virat Kohli's net sessions aren't often as lengthy or even as scientific as what you would find with a Steve Smith or a Marnus Labuschagne. Rarely does he stretch them for over thirty minutes, unless of course he's got a very specific goal in mind. Another quirk about Kohli in the nets is that you rarely see him get too upset with himself, which is unlike every other top batter in the world. From Smith and Labuschagne to Joe Root and Ben Stokes, you're never too far away from a very audible remonstration, with the occasional cuss word thrown in (especially in the case of England's current Test captain).

So to hear Kohli grunt and groan after mistiming a couple of cover drives was perhaps a further sign of how much he was building himself up for his only Test on tour. He was particularly unhappy with his bat face closing on a couple of occasions as he looked to force length deliveries from young Kartik Tyagi. Incidentally, Pujara wasn't too chuffed with himself either as he played a delivery on to his stumps. A few seconds of self-contemplation later, the two premier batters were back working on their game. It was not until some twenty minutes into his session that Kohli whipped a delivery—similar to the one he'd mistimed off Umesh Yadav—with disdain. That was when he started to look happy with himself.

He was also getting the throwdown crew to target him at high speeds in the region between his chest and head. The initial phase of this challenge was more about picking and choosing the deliveries to leave. Those hands stayed up high, like he'd told Agarwal the previous day. There was no way even a ball that behaved in an unruly or unexpected fashion could get close to either his bat or his gloves. He also kept grading every duck and every weave, especially when facing Raghu's thunderous arm.

He never went beyond 'three and a half' out of five. There were to be no let-ups, not against the Aussies. And Kohli didn't mind being his own hardest taskmaster. The occasional 'Shottttyaaaar' would ring out from Shastri every time the captain did get into position and play that customarily ferocious pull shot.

Rathour kept reminding Kohli to make sure his weight wasn't going back too much while leaving balls and also to make sure that his right foot was going across the right distance.

From that point on, Kohli started looking to play and 'score' off the short-pitched deliveries square on the off side, shouting 'one', 'one maybe', 'no run there', based on how well he'd made contact. Next door, Pujara had Nuwan Seneviratne smashing tennis balls at him from close quarters in a bid to strengthen his reflexes. Kohli, generally not one for unconventional techniques, stuck to the more traditional method.

Kohli was so specific with the finer details that when Nuwan hurled a couple of balls from wide of the crease, he shook his head in anger and could be heard telling the throwdown specialist, 'Starc doesn't come from that wide of the crease. Bowl from there,' pointing to the exact spot before telling one of the support staff that he wanted it to be perfect.

By the time Kohli was done with preparing for the Australian pace contingent, it was time for Nathan Lyon—or Sundar morphing into the greatest off spinner Australia have ever produced. The coaching staff had decided to keep Sundar back specifically for that reason.

'There are no net bowlers. We couldn't have had Ash bowling in the nets all the time, he had to be kept fresh for the matches. So we told Sundar to stay back,' a coach recalled at the time.

Sridhar stood in charge of Sundar shouting out instructions in Tamil, with India's T20I regular bowling off-breaks into the faux-rough area that the coaching staff had demarcated on the side of the pitch. Sundar did take a while to get into his groove, and a couple of times, when he ended up pitching the ball closer to Pujara's stumps, the seasoned right-hander clipped away with ease. 'That line, he'll grind you away all day long, man,' Sridhar berated him from behind the batsman. For good measure, the fielding coach did shout, 'Nice one, Garrryy . . .' every time Sundar landed the ball where his coach and senior teammates wanted him to.

India had worked similarly to thwart the Lyon challenge before the start of their previous Test tour to Australia. Back then, they had also utilized a leg slip, with the coaching staff setting challenges to the batsmen to not get struck on the gloves by the top-spin deliveries. They'd go on to do that here too, but to start with, it was all about getting the batters used to playing off the rough.

While Pujara defended, Kohli drove against the turn and from the virtual rough. '*Pace-a maathu, batsman maaritaan* (Change the pace, the batsman has changed),' Sridhar would yell out as Kohli began to find the challenge all too easy.

It led to Sundar putting more body and revs on the ball, but in vain, as Kohli only seemed to enjoy facing him even more. It was Kohli who then asked the youngster to take a break, once he was content with what he wanted to achieve from the unique session.

It was also the setting for a rather fascinating debate on batting ideologies between the two all-time greats of Indian Test cricket. It had to do with their respective approaches to playing spinners in turning conditions.

Off the first few balls Pujara had faced from Sundar, India's Test No. 3 had offered his bat to only a couple, preferring to pad most of the others away. He then did the same to one delivery, which was rather close to the off stump, and was adjudged LBW by umpire Sridhar, who never moved from right behind the stumps. Kohli couldn't hold it in anymore. He decided to indulge his old sparring partner in a healthy exchange.

Kohli: '*Arey ballle se khel . . . itna bada balla hai haath mein* (Use your bat . . . you have such a big bat in your hand).'
Pujara just smiled and ignored his captain's comment.

The next ball from Sundar was full and outside off stump, which Pujara drove forcefully through the cover region. Off went Kohli again.
Kohli: '*Dekha . . . balle se khelega toh kya hota hai* (Did you see that? Look what happens when you use your bat)!'

Pujara, though, was having none of it. He even paused his session briefly and, with a smile on his face, had the final word.

Pujara: '*Last time, yeh hi plan chala tha* (This is the plan that worked for me last time).'

Kohli didn't mind it one bit and laughed it off. With less than ten days to go for his scheduled departure, the Indian captain had only one mission in sight—to have the final word in the opening chapter of what was already shaping up as an epic.

7

Thirty-Six All Out

There was something ominous in the air on 19 December 2020. And you could sense it long before we even got to the Adelaide Oval. Long before India resumed their ill-fated second innings on what was Day Three of the first Test. Long before we witnessed the most unbelievable of batting collapses in Test history.

The minor drawback of your 'home' Test being a day/night contest is that your mornings aren't spent discovering the latest coffee blend at the café down the road or catching up with a colleague for an avocado or vegemite toast. No, instead you wake up with a plethora of household chores to complete.

'The bins won't just walk out, you know,' you are duly informed. 'The car won't get washed by itself,' you are duly reminded. And it was while I was giving our ten-year-old Ford Fiesta a final scrub around noon that the fateful message popped up on the Australian cricket media WhatsApp group. It was from the lovely Lucy Williams. There was nothing lovely about the contents of the message, though. Lucy, who continues to do an incredible job with the incredible Aussie women's team, was in charge of that Test as the venue manager.

'Morning all, we've just been notified that Cronulla 2230 is now a hot spot. Can you please contact me directly if you've been in the area or any of the following surrounding suburbs,' the message read, followed by a dozen or so Sydney postcodes.

The message was directed mainly towards those of us who'd been in Sydney the previous week—on or before 13 December, to be precise. That included a majority of those present in Adelaide, considering we'd mostly all been there for India's second warm-up game at the SCG.

It sent me immediately fumbling through Google, looking up the postcodes, hoping that I hadn't accidentally stumbled within the vicinity of any of those. I also called Gaurav and asked him to rush to the ground. He'd gone to meet a friend for lunch, blissfully unaware of the drama about to unfold at the Adelaide Oval.

I didn't waste much time either and rushed to the ground. The entry into the Adelaide Oval for the first two days had been a very smooth affair. Unlike during normal times, when the media pack enters via the Members' Gates, which can be crowded, we'd been getting in through a side gate next to the lifts that take us to the media centre. It was to further restrict our contact with the rest of the public. This was, after all, the first Test during the pandemic, with the crowd back in attendance.

All you needed to do was to have your mask on and keep your accreditation cards ready to be scanned by the very friendly security personnel. And off you went up to the fourth floor, which houses what I believe are the best facilities for journalists and broadcasters alike in Australia.

It wasn't so straightforward that afternoon, though. For starters, there were a few more people in attendance near the entry point. That included the lady in a hazmat suit, who stood holding a sheet of paper containing a bunch of Sydney postcodes.

'Can you please scan through all of them and let us know if you've been to any of these any time before 13 December?' she asked me. There were a couple of extra entries on that list, compared to the one Lucy had sent an hour or so earlier. Thankfully, I hadn't gone anywhere close to the new hotspots that had sprouted up around the cluster along the northern beaches of Sydney.

'So, what would happen if I had actually been in one of those areas?' I asked her innocently. The matter-of-fact response came without her batting an eyelid: 'Oh, we'd have given you a mask, asked you to stand out there and informed the state health authorities. Then they would have sent a couple of cops over to come take you to an authorized motel, where you'd have had to quarantine for two weeks,' she informed me very casually. To say that it sent a chill down my spine would be an understatement.

I couldn't help but imagine with dread the prospect of being stuck inside a room for that long, especially when you didn't even have the virus. It would have also ended my tour for all practical purposes. This book would have read a lot differently, had there been one to begin with.

Once inside the Oval, I stuck to my usual routine of sneaking to the back to watch the nets before the start of play. In there was Wriddhiman Saha, having a long hit, and I tweeted something about how he could end up playing a big role for India with the bat later in the day. In hindsight, it's safe to say I wasn't totally wrong about it.

The visitors were well on top at this stage of the Test. Sixty-two runs ahead, with nine wickets left, in what was shaping up like a low-scoring contest. Not to forget that Day Three was expected to be the best for batting on what had been a difficult pitch till then for most batters except Virat Kohli.

Out on the ground, meanwhile, nightwatchman Jasprit Bumrah was knocking around, looking more and more confident with every forceful drive. Bumrah the batter still seemed to be riding on the high of his maiden first-class half-century a week earlier in Sydney. And the Indian camp was all smiles and laughter as he walked off to prepare himself to resume his innings from the previous day. There was a confident vibe to them, like they were in control of their own destiny.

Not many could say the same in the media centre, though. By the time I got up there, with only a handful of minutes left for play to commence, the mood had turned chaotic. There were more questions than answers. Some of the Sydney-based journalists had already left, desperate to catch a flight back home and avoid being stuck in Adelaide. Others crowded poor Lucy and her other colleagues at Cricket Australia, trying to get some clarity on what impact the new developments could have on the rest of the series.

It wasn't simply a case of what was happening in Adelaide. The Victorian health authorities had announced earlier that morning that anyone who'd been in the vicinity of Greater Sydney, which includes the SCG, during that period wouldn't be allowed to enter their state after 11.59 p.m. on 20 December, which was technically Day Four of the first Test.

That potentially put the Boxing Day Test in jeopardy for those among us who were planning to go and cover it in Melbourne. Of course, we weren't even considering the prospect of this match not going the distance, let alone finishing on Day Three. And it's safe to say that not many inside the Adelaide Oval press box were focused on the brisk start to the dramatic day's proceedings.

Yes, we did look up to see Mayank Agarwal flick a full delivery on his pads from Mitchell Starc for four in the first over. Yes, we did notice Bumrah not making the most of his form in practice and chipping a ball straight back to Pat Cummins in the second over of the day. But apart from a couple of local journalists, nobody else was really in their designated seat to witness these seemingly ancillary events.

Instead, we were split into many huddles at the back, each contemplating the right move to ensure that we neither got held back in Adelaide nor ended up missing Melbourne. For some it was simply a question of not being put in a position where they'd have to miss Christmas with family. It helped that the three overs that followed Bumrah's dismissal were largely uneventful. Then Cheteshwar Pujara walked out to bat. Surely, Pujara would occupy the crease for a while and let us figure out our next plan of action.

But then off went Pujara, followed right after by Agarwal and Ajinkya Rahane in the same over. India's score suddenly read 15/5. It was only at that point that the hullabaloo in the press box paused briefly as everyone took a deep breath. It was like there was a collective gasp of, 'Wait, is this really happening?' Before anyone could even wrap their heads around it, Kohli was out too. 19/6.

The Indian captain had been surprisingly jittery in this innings, especially in comparison to how sublime he'd looked in the first innings. Maybe, you thought, he had come out with a counterattack in mind. There was nearly an outside edge, an inside edge and a wafty boundary past Cameron Green at gully. Then the flash at a sucker ball wide of the off stump from Pat Cummins, with Green holding on to the catch for dear life. For the second time in three days, Kohli walked back towards the dressing room shaking his head in disbelief. This time, though, he also looked a little shellshocked. He wasn't the only one. We all were.

We'd all witnessed collapses before, but this was different. There were no plays and misses. Only edges and catches. It felt like we'd been transported into a batter's fever dream. It was seam bowling of the highest order, yes. And Pat Cummins and Josh Hazlewood are certain to go down as among the greatest fast bowlers Australia has ever produced. But even they couldn't be so good. Even they couldn't possibly be so unrelenting as to not even let the batter have the satisfaction of being beaten but still having survived. Even they couldn't be producing spells where the batters were made to look so far out of their depth. They were doing all this, though. The Indians weren't just being humbled, they were being decimated.

In the space of 20–25 minutes, the cricketing conversations in the media centre had gone from what kind of target India might set for the home team to whether they could go past the dreaded figure of 26, the lowest Test total of all time. Thankfully, the 7-run partnership between Hanuma Vihari and Saha at least took India on par with that mythical number.

It was around then that Sunil Gavaskar, who was here as a commentator for Channel 7, walked out of the box to inquire about India's lowest total in Test cricket. He'd been the key figure of the batting line-up that had succumbed to 42 at Lord's on 20 June 1974. You couldn't blame him for hoping that this embarrassing statistic—India's lowest Test total—would no longer be associated with him.

Almost on cue, Saha and R. Ashwin were dismissed off two consecutive deliveries. 26/8.

If there ever was a possibility for a batter to get timed out in a Test match, this had to be it. This was the closest you'd get to a batting innings being played out on a conveyor belt. Not to forget that there was but a single review taken, when Ashwin felt like he hadn't edged Hazlewood to Tim Paine behind the stumps. Somehow there wasn't even a single delay, in terms of the batter getting to the crease and marking his guard punctually. Maybe they were in a daze.

Despite the ridiculous score, the stage was set for that inevitable late-order partnership—the kind where the tailenders start edging through gaps and the specialist batter gets a couple of boundaries away. But on this bizarre day, even that wasn't to be. And the insult would end with a terrible injury.

On most days, Mohammed Shami is your classic old-school tailender who prefers getting away from the line of the ball and then swinging his bat at it. That's what he was trying to do here. But Cummins was following him. Shami responded to the first short ball with an untoward swat while on his haunches. He responded in a similar fashion to the next one. Unfortunately, it left him locked up awkwardly, with no room to escape. And when the ball smashed into his right forearm, you knew that was it for Shami. Physio Nitin Patel, who would end up as the unsung hero of the tour, tried everything he could, from taping the arm to using the spray. To Shami's credit, he did seem intent on staying out in the middle. But the fact that he couldn't hold or pick up his bat made his efforts to do so rather futile. India's nightmare had come to a painful end, with the enforcer of their bowling attack seemingly having been knocked out of the equation. A few minutes later this was confirmed, as Shami left the Adelaide Oval with his arm in a sling.

It read 36/9 on the historic scoreboard at the Cathedral End. It was unfathomable. What had just happened here? Gaurav and I walked all the way across the oval to pose for a selfie in front of the scoreboard at the end of the day. We simply had to. Surely, this was a kind of cricketing anomaly we'd never get to witness again.

'In some ways, it felt like watching a TV show where you get the plot, maybe even understand it, but still can't simply get your head around how or why it's unfolding the way it is. And it was done literally before you could even press pause to reread the synopsis.' This was how I described it that day. I still stand by it. I've subsequently watched a few reruns of that finale episode, and it still doesn't feel like it was part of the original plot.

India's abject surrender within the first session on Day Three did allow those of us hoping for a smooth passage to Melbourne to heave a sigh of relief, for very selfish reasons. With Australia needing only 90 to win, we would surely be able to sneak past the Victoria border before midnight the following day. Poor Ian Chappell, though, wasn't allowed to relax. He was, in fact, whisked away from the press box at some point after the lunch break. It mainly had to do with his home being somewhere along Sydney's northern beaches, and his suburb being on the updated 'hotspot' list.

The legendary former Australian captain, and equally legendary raconteur, had spent the lunch break chatting away with Gaurav and me about off spin. He spoke about the difference in the challenges posed by Erapalli Prasanna and Srinivas Venkataraghavan during his playing days; also about the guile of Prasanna, his ability to get the ball to drop on the batter, and made some comparisons with R. Ashwin; and why he'd always found it more comfortable facing Venkataraghavan. To our relief, we were later informed that he'd managed to get a flight out to Sydney rather than having to stay confined in Adelaide for two weeks.

India's unexpected capitulation also brought some relief for the broadcasters, maybe not so much in terms of their TRPs but in terms of the logistics for their commentary teams. Gavaskar had been informed that the Channel 7 crew would be getting the first flight out to Melbourne the following morning. They were also likely to stay back there for the third and fourth Tests, to commentate on those games off TV. It meant that our plans to catch up for lunch in Adelaide and be entertained by one of the foremost storytellers in cricket history were scuppered.

India still had to drag themselves out to the middle to show some spirit. Not surprisingly, they looked as out of it as you'd expect them to be. Their brief foray on the ground was replete with misfields and dropped chances. For once, even the great Virat Kohli didn't have his customary 'glass-half-full' energy to lift his team up. All he could offer at best was a wry smile and continued shaking his head in disbelief every time he caught the '36' on the Adelaide Oval scoreboard.

His final few moments on the 2020–21 tour of Australia more or less summed up the disastrous nature in which it had concluded. Hanuma Vihari made a courageous yet futile effort at fine leg, but the ball slipped through his fingers and went over the ropes. The top edge had come off Joe Burns's bat. The Australian opener had held on to his place on what many believed to be a one-Test-at-a-time probation plan. And the fact that it was Burns who'd see Australia home with an unbeaten half-century after having failed in the first innings put India's shocker of a day further into perspective.

This, clearly, wasn't how Kohli had imagined his trip to Australia would come to an end. While the rest of his teammates staggered towards the two Aussie batters to congratulate them, Kohli stood unmoved in his position at second slip. He kept staring towards the now-empty fine-leg region, but maybe he was just listlessly gazing into the distance. It took Rahane to come all the way over and guide Kohli towards the direction of the Australian dugout for the customary fist bumps. Kohli's attention, though, remained fixated on the big screen at the River End, showing a replay of that final missed opportunity by Vihari. Another dejected shake of the head. This time, his head dropped a tad too, with his eyes on the ground. The reality of the shocking turn of events was sinking in on a day at which Indian cricket will forever shake its head.

It's safe to say that the Aussies couldn't quite believe what had transpired either. They'd started the day on the back foot, with 'damage limitation' on their mind. But here they were a few hours later, as comprehensive winners of the first Test.

Yet, India didn't come across as the villains of the piece. You still felt some sympathy for them. It honestly wasn't the kind of shoddy batting display that deserved the embarrassing outcome. And to think about how promising it all looked going into this opening Test: when Kohli was at his sublime best late on Day One; when they had Australia on the hop at 111/7; when they'd come to the ground that very morning.

★ ★ ★

Neither Kohli nor Pujara faced a single delivery with the pink ball under lights before doing so in the actual game. After opting out of the practice game at the SCG, the two senior batters also chose not to avail the unique facilities at the Adelaide Oval. It is, after all, the only venue in Australia with match-quality lights in the nets area.

It was quite surprising, considering both had come on this tour having played a single day/night Test, in very different conditions, against Bangladesh at the Eden Gardens. Pujara had told me, on the sidelines of the Drummoyne Oval game, about the difficulties in sighting the pink ball once the day's play entered the twilight zone; about how you couldn't really get 'used to' facing it, regardless of how much you'd prepared for it. He'd also concurred with Marnus Labuschagne's take on it, which I'd once overheard in the nets, where Australia's No. 3 had compared playing the pink ball to 'batting in outer space', where the ball almost seemed to be wobbly even if wasn't really moving.

Surely, you thought Pujara at least would want a hit. The crunched nature of the schedule also meant that the only chance India had of doing so was the evening before the Test. The team management clearly weren't prepared to risk exposing one of their key players so close to the opening contest.

'We asked Puji to save all his concentration and focus for the Test. It was a long but compressed tour, so there was no point wasting a lot of energy in the nets,' one of the coaches would tell us later.

Though Rahane did play and captain the team at the SCG, he too barely got any practice for batting under lights. He was caught behind by Alex Carey off Jack Wildermuth just before the sun had started to set in Sydney. It meant that going into India's second-ever day/night Test, only Hanuma Vihari, who scored a classy century in the second innings against Australia A, among the key batters had spent any time batting at night, though Jasprit Bumrah might take umbrage at that statement, considering he did make his maiden first-class half-century while top-scoring in the first innings.

Australia, on the other hand, had the luxury of assembling in Adelaide nearly ten days before the first Test. They'd set up camp there and had several practice sessions under lights in the centre of the Adelaide Oval, with the likes of Smith and Labuschagne making the most of it.

I had returned from Sydney a day earlier, skipping the final day of the pink-ball warm-up game. I'd done so to be home for my wife's birthday on 13 December. I did concede a few of the obligatory 'brownie points' later that evening by hopping into the Adelaide Oval very briefly to catch Tim Paine & Co. go through some of their routines. I stayed for their regulation game of touch rugby under cloudy skies but left before the nets began. I had a birthday dinner to get to, of course. As I was leaving, I saw Justin

Langer walk on to the practice pitches in the middle, alongside the 22 yards being prepared for the match, mark his guard at both ends and start shadow batting. Considering the uncertainty that hung over the home team's opening combination, perhaps the coach had decided to take on the task himself.

A day later, it was confirmed that Langer wasn't making an unexpected comeback to Test cricket. Instead, he was busy making his final choice between the incumbent Joe Burns and Marcus Harris, who had impressed everyone against India on the previous tour. There had been some suggestion that Marnus Labuschagne might get slotted up to open. Thankfully, that idea was shelved quickly.

Burns was first in for a hit during the practice session, two days from the Test, and Langer was right behind him. It was a very hands-on session, as the former Australian opener put the current one through the grind. Langer was fully involved from the very first ball Burns faced, which led the coach to walk into the net for a rather animated chat. This process was repeated a couple of times in a bid to get the right-hander into the best position, especially in terms of where his head was when the ball was being delivered.

But the fired-up duo of James Pattinson and Michael Neser weren't making life any easier for the Queenslander. It took at least a good half hour before Burns started to feel a lot more at ease and in rhythm. By this time, Langer had moved behind the net and was soon beside it, at a square-on position. Burns would return an hour later for another stint in the nets, with his focus now on adding a front-foot press in his load-up at the crease to ensure freer movement both forward and back, without becoming too handsy, which has been an issue for him against the moving ball. And as Australia wrapped up for the day, it seemed confirmed who one of their openers would be.

That Burns would be walking out to open the innings alongside Matthew Wade was an idea out of left field. So much so that even the gritty left-hander from Tasmania wasn't aware that he was being handed a massive promotion in the batting line-up till twenty-four hours before the game.

Wade had put his body on the line rather courageously against the Kiwis the previous summer, letting Neil Wagner, in particular, use his ribs for target practice. Though he didn't quite have the runs to show for it, he'd won the trust of the dressing room and the coaching staff. With the highly talented and highly billed Cameron Green all set to make his Test debut at Wade's erstwhile No. 6 spot, Langer and Paine had decided to show some trust in their ultimate team-man. The plan to have Wade open had been floating ever since Will Pucovski suffered another blow to his head at Drummoyne Oval. Wade would later talk about getting the hint when he noticed his name mentioned on a board alongside the names of top-order batsmen selected to face the Test fast bowlers under lights during the first practice session. The three centre-wicket sessions he had at the Adelaide Oval during the ten-day camp meant that he was as prepared as any of the batters on show for the pink-ball challenge.

India, at least, were sure about one-half of their opening partnership. In Rohit Sharma's absence, Mayank Agarwal was the premier opener in the Test squad. There was no question about his place in the playing eleven, despite his having looked a tad restless at the crease at the SCG. There still remained a question mark over Prithvi Shaw, though. The youngster hadn't really looked his best in the four innings he'd played during the warm-up games. There was the breezy 29-ball 40 at the SCG, but the coaching staff wanted to see a bit more of him in the nets before taking the final call. Maybe some last-minute fine-tuning was required? Contrary to some media reports back in India, there was never a consideration to bring K.L. Rahul in place of Shaw.

While Kohli was his busy self at the nets, either batting or dishing out throwdowns to some of the tailenders, the coaches' attention seemed to be more on Shaw. Shastri, in particular, was in the young opener's ear a lot about getting his body more in line with the ball. He seemed to be asking him to add a little back-and-across movement as a trigger in his stance. It was Shastri's bid to get Shaw more aware of where his off stump was, in order to limit the number of times he flashed at deliveries that he ideally could leave alone. Shaw did play one on to his stumps. Luckily for him, it was when Shastri wasn't watching.

Agarwal, meanwhile, was engrossed in a session with batting coach Vikram Rathour, trying to implement some of the tips he'd picked from Kohli in Sydney. He still seemed to be coming up a bit short, literally, in terms of being able to contend with the extra lift off the surfaces in Australia. While he plugged away, Shastri was seen exhibiting, to Shaw and Shubman Gill, the perfect position to tackle the bounce, which involved pressing forward a lot more than you would in England.

Shaw returned later, this time to bowl his leg spin, which he had a lot of confidence in. He insisted on having taken a 'panja', or a five-wicket haul, the last time he'd been called on to bowl in a competitive match. And he did manage to turn a few balls viciously past Wriddhiman Saha. With Ravindra Jadeja ruled out, India seemed desperate to find a fifth bowling option to manufacture the balance they'd ideally have had if the all-rounder had been fit enough to play.

For the record, T. Natarajan was the most impressive of the bowlers during the practice sessions, troubling every single Indian batter.

Kuldeep Yadav bowled a long spell under the watchful eyes of Bharat Arun, who kept encouraging the wrist spinner to focus on his speeds. His body language was suggestive that he wasn't in line for a surprise call-up. It was not really the best week for Kuldeep. His response to Gaurav's query about what he had been up to on his birthday, on 14 December, was pretty self-deprecatory. Let's just say it wasn't the poor fellow's best birthday ever.

R. Ashwin was visibly excited about his impending battle with Smith. He was one of the only two members from the playing

XI to make it for the optional session on the eve of the Test. He spent most of it in conversation with Arun, explaining the fields he wanted to set for his arch-rival and the shots he expected him to play. He also explained to Arun the many ways he could picture himself getting Smith out. He then entered the nets and started practising the deliveries he'd need to execute his myriad plans.

There was a minor concern in the Australian camp about Smith's fitness, to the extent that we were all on Smith watch for an hour or so before he was finally spotted marking his guard in the practice area. It was a back spasm, we were told. It's something that still dogs him occasionally. You'd see the ace batter stretching his back on certain days while at the nets. In December 2020, it kept him from taking part in any of the team's pre-net routines on the days leading up to the Test, even if he did sneak in a batting session on both days.

Wanting to make the most of whatever time they had, Damian Hough, the Adelaide Oval's fantastic head curator, had managed to get the drop-in pitches in place and ready despite being extremely taxed. Firstly, due to the State of Origin rugby game—the New South Wales vs Queensland battle—and then due to the sudden Covid lockdown in Adelaide. Hough, of course, had famously got the centre square ready in two days' time after the rock band AC/DC had left the Oval 'Thunderstruck' a couple of years earlier. This time around, though, Hough could only put half of the twelve pitches on the square and decided to leave 8 mm grass on the 22 yards being used for the match. Based on his reading of the surface, Hough expected the ball to skid a lot more but not to nip around too much, as had been the case for some years with the pink ball.

★ ★ ★

You wonder when the reality of a run-out really sinks in for the perceived 'guilty party' in a mix-up. The moment they realize that they've made the wrong call? The moment they realize they've sold their partner down the river? The moment they realize their partner's haplessness as he or she turns around and gives them that despondent look before walking off? Or the moment they realize the potential repercussions of their error?

For Ajinkya Rahane, it seemed to sink in pretty quickly. To call it a blunder would be stretching it, though. It wasn't so much poor judgement of the run as it was a misjudgement of how well he'd timed the ball, off Nathan Lyon's bowling, while pushing it towards mid-off. The call was also instinctive. It didn't help that the non-striker, Kohli, was someone who's probably among the most eager in the world when it comes to responding to a call. Nor the fact that the Indian captain is someone who jets off at full tilt always. It was over in less than a second. 'Yes. No. Oh nooo . . .'

As Kohli walked off, shaking his head in dismay and chucking his gloves away before entering the tunnel, Rahane knew the momentum of the game had changed. Later, in subsequent interviews, he would admit having felt that way too. India were placed perfectly, with the lights having now taken full effect at the Adelaide Oval. At 188/3, they were in a position to boss the early phase of this Test. Most importantly, Kohli had walked out to bat in 'legend' mode. All that effort and focus he'd put into preparing for his only Test on tour was coming to fruition now. He'd spent the time down in the dugout, before his turn to bat, shadow batting and virtually facing two out of every five deliveries that were bowled in the middle. It felt like he was already set by the time he walked out to bat.

The initial phase of his innings was all about attrition, choosing the right balls to leave—and he left quite a few of them as Cummins and Hazlewood kept coming at him. The first boundary of his innings came only when he faced the 45th delivery. It was classic Kohli, trying to put Nathan Lyon under pressure by dancing down the pitch and lofting him over the mid-on, which the off spinner had kept halfway back to the boundary after a lengthy consultation with his captain. The shot immediately brought about a change, with that fielder being pushed back to the boundary. Kohli and Lyon seemed to be loving the contest as always, constantly in each other's ear but mostly in a friendly fashion. 'I know you'll love that,' he was overheard telling Lyon at one stage over the stump mic, when asked to step out of his crease more often.

To put Kohli's discipline into perspective—he didn't attempt one of his trademark cover drives till the 145th ball of his innings. And he didn't seem too bothered by the fact that it went straight to a fielder. There were plenty of opportunities for him to have done so earlier. But he kept resisting.

He did not hesitate, however, from playing shots at the short-pitched deliveries that came his way, regardless of whether they were from Mitchell Starc or the other two right-arm pacers. His pull and hook shots, too, were a lot more controlled, with the master batter very consciously trying to roll his wrists down a lot more to keep the ball along the ground, even if it meant that on a couple of occasions he ended up playing a double-handed tennis smash.

Rahane had walked out and, as was generally the case when the two batted together on Australian soil, he took over as the aggressor, especially against Lyon. As always, the vice-captain was taking the pressure off his skipper. Rahane had started taking the attack to the Aussie bowlers. There were sweeps and drives off Lyon, and even a top-edged six off Cummins over fine leg. The lights were on, but so were Kohli and Rahane. And when the Indian captain produced, arguably, the shot of the day, by opening up his front foot and driving Lyon inside-out through extra cover for four, Australia were feeling the pinch. Kohli and Rahane had already put on 88 runs at nearly 3 an over, and most of the runs had come during the most difficult batting period of a pink-ball Test: the twilight zone.

You can always make out from the fielding team's reaction whether or not they think they've earned the run-out. If they had induced it by keeping the lid on the batting team for an extended

period, or if they had created it through some magic on the field.
But here, neither had they managed to put the Indians under
pressure, nor had Hazlewood moved too far or too quickly to
chuck the ball to Lyon at the bowler's end. The prize wicket had
been handed to them on a platter. As some of the Aussies would
admit later, they were running out of ideas on how to get Kohli
out. No wonder there was a lot of relief amid the sheer delight in
the Australian camp as Kohli stood staring at Rahane, who put his
hand up apologetically.

Rahane had realized the enormity of the moment all right. So
much so that he looked shaken by the gaffe to such an extent that
he completely played the wrong line of a very full ball from Starc,
with the second new ball, to be trapped LBW. Hanuma Vihari's
efforts to convince him to take the review were met with a blank
expression, and Rahane walked off with his head still hanging low.
In the Indian dressing room, Kohli sat with his eyes glazed over and
still shaking his head.

★ ★ ★

India's dramatic loss in Adelaide would be attributed to the shocking
collapse the following day, and so it should. But for those involved
in the contest, and the ones in the dressing room, you wondered
whether they would rue the missed opportunities of Day Two a
lot more.

For, the visitors had held a vice-like grip on the Aussies for a
major part of the day before letting it slip, around the time they had
done the same with the Kohli run-out twenty-four hours earlier.
While the opening day might not have finished as well as they'd
have hoped for, India still found themselves in a decent position
by stumps. Even Kohli had regained his smile by the end of the
night and had walked down to the sidelines to greet the overnight
batters, Ashwin and Saha.

The next afternoon, he walked out with a tennis racquet
and, after smashing a few balls at the tailenders, as part of their

warm-up session, indulged in an impromptu game of tennis with
K.L. Rahul at the Adelaide Oval. He put Jasprit Bumrah through
the wringer too, with a crash course on facing the short ball, one
that the fast bowler enjoyed a lot. It earned him a batting promotion
too, perhaps, as he got to walk in at No. 10, ahead of Mohammed
Shami. Rahane still didn't seem to have recovered from the run-
out misadventure, and Shastri took him aside with an arm over his
shoulder for a little chat.

Australia didn't take too long to polish off the Indian lower
order. The Indian bowlers, though, made the first innings total
of 244 feel a lot bigger. Bumrah and Shami were at their incisive
best, and Umesh Yadav, who'd impressed in the warm-up games,
backed them up just the way Kohli would have wanted him to.

Bumrah had really made his first major impression as a Test
bowler in Australia on the previous tour. Here he was two years
on, better and even more menacing. And it didn't take him long
to knock over the openers, who somehow had managed to survive
the opening assault.

Australia weren't being allowed to get going at all as the
innings progressed. The scoring rate was kept below 2 an over.
Kohli was loving it. He was getting into it, too. After posting
himself at second slip for the first ten overs, he moved over to
mid-off, to be closer to his bowlers and avoid having to walk over
a few times every over.

The man who really put the chokehold on the Aussies, though,
was Ashwin. He had produced one of his best overseas bowling
performances at the same venue in 2018. But as I saw him warm
up in between innings, his cap still on, the only thought in my head
was whether he'd do a Greg Matthews and keep his headgear on
while bowling, like he had at the Drummoyne Oval. Much to our
disappointment, he did not.

To nobody's surprise, all that preparation and planning he had
put in was beginning to show right from the moment he got the
ball in his hands. As did the ideas he had discussed with Bharat
Arun about getting Steve Smith out.

Writing for Cricbuzz, this was how I had described the 'spin scientist's Eureka moment':

To understand the essence of how Smith was cornered, it's important to focus on the two deliveries leading to his dismissal. For, it's with these two that Ashwin not only set his man up, but also showcased his next level of evolution as a world-class spinner. On both occasions, Smith stretched forward to defend the ball. On both occasions, he realised he wasn't quite to the pitch of the ball. On both occasions, the ball dipped and landed just that bit shorter than where Smith had expected it to. The master batsman did however have enough time to adjust enough to keep them out. Having been beaten by the length twice in a row, Smith's natural reaction was to then stay back in his crease for the third delivery and look to negate it off the backfoot. But here's where the other characteristic of the top-spinning delivery came through as it bounced just that little more upon pitching, and eventually caught the splice of the bat en route to Ajinkya Rahane for his umpteenth grab off Ashwin's bowling.

This dismissal had also set in motion one of the more underrated series rivalries between two exceptional cricketers, which would keep getting more competitive as we moved towards Melbourne and Sydney.

We've seen Ashwin weave his magic on Indian pitches for over a decade now. But what he did at the Adelaide Oval that evening was add that Ashwin flavour to this foreign concoction, leaving the Aussies both shaken and stirred.

There had been the customary chatter around Ashwin's numbers in Australian conditions before the series. And also about whether he'd be able to generate the kind of overspin that Lyon had been utilizing to dominate Test cricket down under since 2011. We saw Ashwin try out a few tweaks at the Drummoyne Oval, where he seemed to have added an exaggerated flourish in his load-up. His right elbow had started to push back before he entered his final release motion. Perhaps it was just to make sure he cocked his wrists to then help him come from a little more over the top, to accentuate the overspin. And not to forget, to arm the slightly bent middle finger that he utilizes to enable the top spin. It wasn't so pronounced in Adelaide, but it was still working wonders. 'It felt like I was making my debut again,' he'd say at the end of the day. I couldn't have put it better. He did seem like someone who'd found a new lease of life.

Travis Head was his next victim, being beaten by that loop and dip, completely befuddled by the eventual length of the ball. In contrast, Cameron Green, in his first Test innings, went back to a ball that pitched and rushed through, cramping and forcing him to hasten his attempt at a pull shot. The ball came off the top of his bat and was brilliantly snared by Kohli at short mid-wicket. It was a special effort from the captain and one that sums up his approach to cricket.

'He's always worried about the ball bouncing in front of him. When a ball is chipped in the air like that, it should never fall short of mid-wicket. Virat's emphasis is always on making sure he's coming forward, but in that scenario to take a catch behind him was almost going against what he backs himself to do, which makes it even more special than it was,' one of the coaching staff would tell us later.

Marnus Labuschagne, who was having his own fascinating battle with Ashwin, had survived two straightforward dropped catches and fought his way to 47. With Smith getting out cheaply, it was while bowling to Labuschagne that India really began to exhibit the leg theory that they had come to Australia with, and began to reap the benefits that they'd expected to gain from it. Labuschagne was finally knocked over, as was Cummins, and the Australian innings was in disarray.

At 111/7, the hosts were on the cusp of handing India a sizeable lead.

And when Paine got a top edge to an attempted hook shot off Bumrah, who'd targeted the Aussie captain with the short-pitched strategy, the end seemed near. But Mayank Agarwal misjudged the trajectory of the ball, and let it slip through his fingers and over the ropes. Just like with the run-out the previous evening, India had, instead of seizing the moment, let it slip.

Paine had spent a copious amount of time working on his batting during the Sheffield Shield hub in Adelaide a month or so before this series. I'd noticed him staying back for hour-long sessions at the Karen Rolton Oval, long after his Tasmanian teammates had left for the day. He'd also received a lot of technical tips, mostly warranted, from Labuschagne, which he'd put to use while scoring a rare first-class ton against the South Australians.

When his team had their backs against the wall, Paine decided to start batting 'like a wicket-keeper', a piece of advice he'd received from Ian Healy on the previous Ashes tour. He began to counterattack and, despite not receiving much support from the other end, began to rattle the Indians. The lengths that had been impeccable throughout the day now suddenly began to falter, and he made sure to make full use of every scoring opportunity. The boundaries started to flow, and, as happens so often in low-scoring matches, he managed to close the gap significantly, dragging Australia closer than they'd thought possible to that Indian total. He eventually ended up playing one of the most influential knocks of his Test career. His unbeaten 73 hadn't just limited the damage, it had given Australia hopes of staying in the contest. But with India now left with two and a half sessions of daylight to bat under on Day Three, they still held all the aces. Or so we thought.

As we know now, the game was over before the sun had even set on this lovely summer evening in Adelaide, before the floodlights around the Adelaide Oval had even started to warm up. Courtesy of a batting performance that would feature right at the top on Indian cricket's wall of shame.

★ ★ ★

Once done with our scoreboard selfie, we waited for the team to leave. To be honest, our focus was on catching a glimpse of Kohli walking away. We weren't the only ones. Legendary photographer Philip Brown was there too, doing what he does best. And he was perfectly placed alongside us near the Victor Richardson gate to catch the Indian players exiting the Adelaide Oval.

We were surprised how quickly the players exited the dressing room. It meant, perhaps, that the team hadn't been given any sort of dressing-down. There was no outright show of dejection, whether it be bowed heads or slouched shoulders. They looked disappointed, but the reactions weren't extreme. It was more a bad day at the office than the end of the world.

Kohli was among the last to leave, on the phone, still looking a bit astonished. A handful of Indian fans were lingering around, somehow having evaded the security guards. They even let the Indian captain know that they still 'loved him'. Kohli glanced very briefly at them before disappearing under the stand with his phone clutched to the right ear. Gaurav and I wondered semi-seriously whether he was on a call with his travel agent to see if he could get the earliest flight out of Adelaide that night itself. As it turned out, he did stay back for another night to do his best as captain to lift the spirits of the deflated unit he was leaving behind. He was even spotted having coffee with Jasprit Bumrah the next morning at a café not too far from the team hotel while some of the younger members in the squad took a ride around the city on electric scooters.

In a sweet moment captured right before the teams parted ways, Tim Paine walked up to his counterpart on the sidelines of the post-match presentation to have a quick friendly chat. Maybe a word of congratulations in advance. It was good to see Test match rivalries taking a back seat and real life taking over. For now, though, that was that. Kohli was gone, and in many people's opinions, so were India.

As both of us headed for the exit at the Adelaide Oval, we spotted the ground staff, including head curator Damian Hough.

Were they surprised by the way India folded on that pitch? Did they expect the pitch to behave in that manner?

Day Three was probably the first time the pitch got a real baking. Perhaps that was why the pitch quickened up in that first session. 'To be honest, we were slightly disappointed with the lack of pace in it during the first couple of days. But that was purely due to the cold weather,' one of them explained. It all seemed to make sense, but the way India fell apart still didn't. Neither for us nor for them.

The premature finish also gave Gaurav and me the chance to have a proper sit-down dinner, a rarity during a day/night Test. And as we tucked into our kway teow noodles and pandan chicken, we spotted Rishabh Pant and Shubman Gill walk into the same restaurant, Lemongrass Thai Bistro, looking for a table in a 'private' area. Not a great idea for a Saturday night on Rundle Street. They were politely sent on their way. It was in keeping with how it had played out for the Indian cricketers in Adelaide on 19 December 2020. Walk in and walk out while barely being noticed and with nothing to show for it.

8

Rahane the Captain, Rahane the Leader

It is the night before the fourth Test against Australia in 2017. The series is level at one all. India must, in Dharamshala, try to claim back the Border–Gavaskar Trophy. The task has been made even tougher with the news that Virat Kohli has been ruled out due to a shoulder injury.

Inside the luxury resort at the foothills of the Himalayas, Kohli walks up to Ajinkya Rahane and wishes him all the best for his Test captaincy debut. The two then enter a meeting with the coaching staff.

Anil Kumble, the head coach, begins to discuss the possible combinations with Rahane. With Kohli by his side, Rahane promptly asks, '*Virat Bhai, aap ko kya lagta hai* (What do you think, Virat Bhai)?' The reply from Kohli is blunt but fair: 'It is not about me. This is your team. You will lead the team on the field, so you make the decision.'

Having got Kohli's backing, Rahane doesn't hesitate in putting forth his ideas. He tells the coaching staff that he wants to play five bowlers, so that the team can take the twenty wickets required to win the Test. It becomes very clear to those present that the thought of a draw and playing safe doesn't even cross Rahane's mind. And how steadfast he is when it comes to the approach he wants to take as captain. Furthermore, he lets Kumble & Co.

know that in Kohli's absence, he will bat at No. 4 and take the responsibility of scoring the 'additional' runs.

The five-bowler strategy works, as India defeat Australia to claim the series. Rahane scores a crucial 46, takes five catches and justifies his brief promotion to the top job, even impressing Kohli along the way.

But it is the manner in which he finishes that match that will go on to define Rahane's ability to separate his personality off the field with what you get once he's on the field, especially as a leader.

'We needed 120-odd to win and had lost two quick wickets. Rahane came out and smashed Cummins all over the ground. This was Rahane the leader. The last thing he wanted was for the pressure to build and the dressing room to get tense, so he took it upon himself. He went outside of his comfort zone for the sake of his teammates,' recalled a member of the dressing room from that famous day in Dharamshala.

The right-hander from Mumbai would remain unbeaten at 38 from 27 balls. Having led from the front on every day of the Test, Rahane now was put on the spot by his counterpart Steve Smith, who wanted the Indian players, as they shook hands after the game, to come across to the Australian dressing room to celebrate what had been a hard-fought series.

Rahane didn't even pause; his reply was instantaneous. 'I will need to check with Virat in the dressing room, as I'm only the stand-in skipper. Kohli is the still the captain of the group.' It said everything you need to know about Rahane. He'd truly felt like his responsibility as leader had concluded the minute the on-field battle had ended. Now, the reins were well and truly back with Kohli.

In Australia, he didn't have to come in for Kohli but had to take over from Kohli. That too at a time when India had been embarrassed in the first Test, had lost one of their strike bowlers in Shami and had lost their pride.

Kohli's departure also seemed to convince people in Australia and back home that the team was left with nobody to lift them up after the Adelaide debacle. 'Surely, Rahane couldn't be the guy who could do that,' seemed to be the most common take wherever you looked. Though he'd been around for nearly a decade in international cricket, people in Australia wanted to know more about Rahane—if he'd be capable of not just stepping into Kohli's shoes but walking in them.

Those who have known Rahane for a while knew he was neither going to change nor imitate Kohli. Whatever he was going to do, he was going to do it the Rahane way. The outlook summed up Rahane, the person and the cricketer: seemingly cautious and timid on the outside, but deep down confident in his own ability as a player and leader.

That's Rahane for you. You look back at his junior cricket days, and it was the same. It didn't help that he was in the same batch as Kohli and Ravindra Jadeja. Not surprisingly, he didn't manage to catch anyone's eye, and it was always put down to his body language. The runs still flowed off the bat, but he wasn't flamboyant enough nor seemed to have the personality that stood out. He was always the studious child who went about acing his exams but just never had enough going for him otherwise to get recognized over and above that. Through no fault of his own, of course.

The only time those around Rahane had seen him become emotional and desperate was when he didn't make it to the India Under-19 World Cup team in 2006. He would come to grips with it soon, and it would become an early lesson for him to not deviate from what really made him click—the innate belief in continuing to be who he is regardless of the outcome.

Rahane's drive to keep himself away from the spotlight also came through in how he lived his life away from the field. Even if it meant having to deal with constant jibes from some of his teammates. Like his decision to keep staying in Mulund, a middle-class suburb on the boundary of Greater Mumbai. Rahane did so because he wanted to be close to his parents and live in the neighbourhood where he felt comfortable and could be himself.

And whenever the topic of Rahane preferring to stay away from the plusher suburbs—where others with his credentials had based themselves—came up in the Mumbai dressing room, an Indian teammate and close friend of his would always chip in: 'Ajju living in Bandra or Juhu or South Mumbai? Are you mad? He is typical Marathi *maanus* [person]. The most upper-class place he will move to is Dadar near Shivaji Park. It is the only place where Ajju will fit in.' In fact, Rahane does reside in Dadar nowadays. There were others who would make fun of Rahane's choices—his car, his clothes—but he would remain undeterred.

Ever since the Mumbai Cricket Academy was established at the Bandra Kurla Complex (BKC), it became the place where cricketers from all competitive levels would end up for a hit or some training. There were, of course, always special privileges if you were an India cricketer.

Generally, the procedure was for the player to make specific requests for types of bowlers or bowling machines to the academy a day before. Often, you would have youngsters travelling over two hours on a crowded Mumbai train just to get the opportunity to bowl to the likes of Rahane. As the story goes: once, Rahane had almost reached the academy when he found that he would have to head back for an urgent family matter. Instead of just leaving, he made it a point to meet the net bowlers, who'd come all the way just for him, and spent some time chatting with them, even posing for pictures, before apologizing sincerely and heading off.

As he left, he would tell one of the staff in Marathi, '*Konache nuksaan nako hoyla* (Don't want anyone to feel bad).'

Once, when sledged by an Australian bowler, Rahane was urged by his teammate to give it back. The best Rahane could come up with was to roll his tongue, slip it out of his mouth and make an '*uuuu*' sound. It was a bizarre reaction that encapsulated Rahane's personality. He was never going to be as expressive as Kohli or dominate the screen like Rohit does.

What works in Rahane's favour is that he's never been fazed by the outside noise. He won't be the first cricketer to have that said about him. But in his case, it's always true. His penchant for dead-batting questions that he doesn't feel comfortable answering, even if they might not be controversial in nature, may have made him slightly unpopular in certain media circles. But regardless of whether he's been under the pump or in form, he's never let that guard down. You ask him about a certain ex-cricketer constantly criticizing him, and he would talk about how he only cares for the support of his teammates.

It's the same when it comes to talking about himself. I will confess to having sent him a message a few days before the Boxing Day Test, asking him for some suggestions on whom I could talk to for some background on his leadership. 'Arey you only decide and talk to anyone,' was his reply. It wasn't very helpful from my perspective, but it said a lot about Rahane the man and how uncomfortable he can be when it comes to talking about himself.

It's only apt, then, that what really announced his arrival, making it clear for some of his battle-hardened opponents in Ranji Trophy cricket that Rahane was ready for the next stage, was the sound of the ball coming off his bat during a particular season, and not Rahane having to talk himself up. It was during a Ranji Trophy quarterfinal in Baroda, in early 2011. I sat having coffee with the likes of Murali Kartik, J.P. Yadav and Sanjay Bangar—guys who'd seen hundreds of cricketers come and go in their time. When I asked them about where they thought Rahane stood in terms of India selection, considering the amount of runs he'd scored in the previous few seasons, they almost said in unison that 'he was ready' and that it was the sound you heard when he was timing the ball that season that had convinced them.

Those who have played under him rave about how supportive he is in good and bad times. Ask him about why he is never seen getting angry with a bowler not executing a plan properly or doing a misfield, and he'll tell you, '*Chidoon kaay faayda* (What's the point of getting annoyed)? I find by remaining calm, the mind is at peace, and you end up making better decisions. If you struggle to keep hold of your emotions, then it will be difficult to manage others.'

There are plenty of examples that stand out about Rahane's generosity as both player and person, and why he seems so comfortable to be in charge of a team. 'I remember treating him in the team medical room once, and another player walked in with some sort of pain. Before I could say something, Rahane was quick to suggest he was content to continue with the treatment on his own, and I should give preference to the other player's injury,' a member of the fitness staff told us. 'Rahane knows that cricket won't define him, his personality will. People just say this, but he really believes in it. But that's just him. That's why people don't know much about him. He's happy to be like that. He is just the ultimate team man.'

This quality of his has come through on many occasions during the course of a match too. For example, consider his partnership with Kohli at the MCG in 2014, the day he really showed both his game awareness as well as his ability to take his game up a notch. It was also the performance that led to his really winning over Kohli, potentially putting Rahane in the prime spot to become vice-captain later on.

Rahane is someone who's always believed in visualization. He had visualized pulling, hooking and driving the Australian attack all around the MCG. When he walked out to bat, his mind was flowing with these positive thoughts. When Kohli asked him how he was feeling, he's learnt to have said, 'I feel really positive and feel like taking the game on.' Kohli's reply was, 'Then do it. Don't hesitate. If you are thinking cover drive, then go for it. If you doubt yourself, you will go half-hearted and risk getting caught in the slips. If you are confident and positive, then the ball will go thought the covers for four.' And it did. Rahane took on a fired-up Mitchell Johnson and produced a counterattack, really establishing himself as one of the mainstays of India's Test middle order for a long time to come.

★ ★ ★

Gaurav and I happened to be around at the flat we were sharing in London during the 2017 Champions Trophy when one of our housemates decided to throw Rahane a birthday party. He seemed very touched by the gesture and enjoyed being in our company, and then the time came for him to say something special for the camera. And all he could offer was a 'jhakaas', much to the chagrin of his wife, Radhika, who demanded that he say something more. It wasn't the first time he'd been asked in jest by Radhika to impose himself a lot more and bring his personality to the forefront.

Truth be told, though, that's exactly what he was doing that night, and what he has done throughout his career. He's never bothered about living up to anyone else's expectation, and he doesn't expect those who played under him to do so either.

This was how I'd summed up his captaincy credentials before the MCG Test:

> With Rahane, it's not always been about what he's done on the field but often about how he's done it or how everyone watching him feels he should have done it. As if being the Ajinkya Rahane who's scored more tough runs in more challenging conditions than any other Indian batsman of his generation just isn't enough. He could have always shown more attitude while doing so, right?

It was this ability to shut out all external influences and getting his players to focus solely on doing their jobs right that really turned the corner for India after Adelaide. It also helped that the team management was very much sold on the idea that he was the perfect man to help execute their masterplan once Kohli left.

'Before we embarked on the tour, we knew Virat was going to play one Test. Since Ajinkya was the vice-captain, he was also part of all the initial meetings. So, any strategies we had in mind, he had heard about them. So Virat left and there was no transition required,' said Bharat Arun. 'The fact that Rahane had played so much cricket with the other senior players was always going to help. If you have a look, Rahane, Pujara, Ashwin, Jadeja—they are all the same age. They had played a lot of cricket together from youth tours to India A, so it always helps when you know the other players for close to ten years. You know how they react or stand up to pressure. I believe that helped Rahane lead this team.'

The way Rahane addressed the team after the debacle of Adelaide and the messages he conveyed to the youngsters was significant in India's turnaround.

During the first day of the second Test match, Rahane told Siraj, who was making his debut, to simply enjoy the moment: 'There will be times when you'll go to fine leg and be disappointed with the over or the ball or yourself. When that happens, simply look up around at the big stands and the crowd around you. Just remember when you were growing up dreaming to play for India at the MCG against Australia. All your dreams have come true, so rather than getting irritated, learn to enjoy the moment and be happy where you are.'

To some of the other youngsters who had yet to experience Test cricket, Rahane's message was the same: 'Just imagine you are playing in a Ranji Trophy game. Don't think we're playing against Australia in their backyard, and give yourself a chance to get overawed. Don't be worried about what happens, just live in the moment, and don't overthink or put pressure on yourself. We, as seniors, will look after that.'

A member of the support staff recalled how it was the calm demeanour of Rahane, along with his ability to not let anyone feel the burden of the situation, that enabled players to be in a good mental space. 'I can't recall if he ever said "this is our goal today" or "this session" or "this series". It was more about keeping it simple and letting the junior players have that freedom.'

'He is a very observant person on the cricketing field. You may feel he is not looking at you, but he is aware of your body language and how you are feeling,' says one long-time teammate.

Even in his first Test as captain, at Dharamshala, he stood at first slip and watched Kuldeep Yadav slice through the middle order. He was ecstatic, but at the same time he could observe that Ashwin looked slightly aloof standing at mid-on. At the end of the over, he ran to his senior teammate, put his arm around him, almost to reinforce Ashwin's self-belief, telling him that he was still his premier spinner. A couple of overs later, Ashwin removed Steve Smith on 111 and changed the course of the innings.

During the tour match at the Drummoyne Oval, while standing at gully, Rahane had observed the young and quick Kartik Tyagi was getting agitated with his run-up. A ball later, Rahane ran 50 metres to stand aside Tyagi to give him the self-assurance that every young cricketer needs.

A member of the support staff, who has been in many international dressing rooms globally and was also a part of the Indian team when Rahane had led in previous matches, said, 'I have been fortunate to be a part of many teams in my career, and I can say that Rahane is one of those very rare captains who will not allow his form with the bat to dictate how he captains the side.'

He always wants his team to stay in the present. The day after the MCG victory, Rahane allowed the players to soak in the victory but ensured that all the positive energy was directed towards the rest of the series. 'We still have two Tests to play. Let us keep enjoying playing together,' he told them.

Similarly, at the end of Day Three in Brisbane—after Washington Sundar and Shardul Thakur's partnership had lifted the spirits of the team, and the feeling began to crystalize that regardless of the result, this team had already overachieved—Rahane's message was still the same: 'Two more days to go, boys. Enjoy the journey and stay in the present.'

Eventually, it would end up as a legacy-defining month and a half in Australia for Rahane and his Indian team. Not that it changed Rahane one bit. Not that it made him look at life any differently. Not that it made him look at the Australians any differently.

Forever mindful of not hurting anyone's sentiments, among the first things Rahane did upon getting back home was to politely refuse cutting a cake that his apartment complex had arranged for a welcome ceremony. Simply because it had a kangaroo made of icing on top. He felt it might come across as insulting to the Australians.

9

Redemption at the 'G

Ajinkya Rahane simply could not sleep. It was 2 a.m. on 27 December 2020. The Indian captain was experiencing muscle spasms in the back. After a few restless movements, he felt like he needed a distraction. And he decided to turn his iPad on to watch the highlights of Sachin Tendulkar's exhilarating century against Australia at the MCG on India's 1999–2000 tour to Australia. He ended up watching the highlights of that special knock not once or twice, but several times.

The next morning, Rahane was padded up and seated inside the dressing room above the concourse at the MCG. At ground level in the Indian dugout, Hanuma Vihari also had all his batting gear on. Vihari had batted at No. 4 in both the warm-up matches, and it seemed imminent that he would be the next batter to enter the cauldron.

Soon enough, there was a loud roar around the MCG as Pat Cummins got rid of the well-set Shubman Gill. Our eyes naturally turned towards Vihari in the dugout, but when he didn't even move our gaze shifted a bit further left and caught the sight of Rahane striding out with purpose from the dressing-room tunnel.

The stage was set for him to impose himself on the scene and the series. And to do so in conditions much more in favour of the bowlers than they had been in Adelaide. Not to forget, it was now

Rahane's task to find a way to help his team recover from that face-losing defeat.

It was also like he'd been transported back to 1999, but instead of Tendulkar it was Rahane walking out to bat at the MCG. The sky was cloudy, as on that day twenty-two years ago, and Cummins & Co. had a spring in their stride, just like McGrath & Co. had back then. The pitch was still offering plenty, and the way Rahane would handle the situation would define the series. Just like Tendulkar, the captain, had done in 1999, it was Rahane the batter/leader who bailed India out of trouble, finishing unbeaten on 104.

It was an innings that laid a marker for his team's character to not bow down when the going gets tough. It was also a statement that they would give it back to the Aussies but do it in his way.

The day would end in a dramatic fashion, with debris flying all over the MCG due to a gale blowing around the ground accompanied by heavy rain. Rahane had been struck on the glove, or so it looked like, in front of his helmet, as he tried fending off a snorter from Mitchell Starc, only for Travis Head to make a meal of it. Then, off he went with the rest of the players.

The next morning at breakfast, Shastri would walk up to his captain, flash a big thumbs-up at him and go, 'That was an innings and a half.' He couldn't have put it better.

Rahane's unique and unplanned individual preparation in the wee hours, watching the highlights of Tendulkar's innings at the same venue, had paid off. But on a larger scale, it was the way Rahane and the coaching staff prepared the team after the debacle of Adelaide that ensured this tour wouldn't fizzle out like had many before and like the experts had predicted.

★ ★ ★

'SHIT HAPPENS!'

That was pretty much the key message from Ravi Shastri to the Indian dressing room at the Adelaide Oval as they sat trying to wrap their heads around the humiliating collapse earlier in the day.

According to some of the players present in the room that evening, this was what Shastri told them: 'I don't want us to talk about that second innings. Let me say that it was superb bowling, and God was also in the Australian dressing room. In my forty years of cricket, I've never seen—no play and misses—just edges and that too going to slips or keeper. What I do want to talk about is those first two days where we were terrific and bloody competitive. We know, and the Aussies also know that if we post 250–300, they are in for a tough time. We bowled superbly, and the bowling plans have worked. The runs will come. We outplayed them for two days, but shit happened in that one hour. Go back to the rooms and don't think too much. We will gather tomorrow.'

'There was no point dwelling too much upon what had happened right at the moment. They are elite sportsmen, of course they will be disappointed. Sometimes you just have to let it sink in and then construct a plan on how to work on it. No point overthinking it straightaway, because there are so many thoughts and emotions that go through your head at that time,' Bharat Arun explained to us during a recent conversation.

One of the first elements the team management wanted to focus on was the players' mindset. They didn't want any negativity clogging their minds and run the risk of doubts resurfacing. Importantly, as Shastri had said in his post-match address, they wanted to deviate the attention of the players from the third day's play. So, the coaching staff decided to gather the players around in the hotel for dinner and a mix of various games like charades.

'It ended up being a great evening. All the team members were there until late. It was a fun night. If anyone from outside had seen the team that night, people would have been saying, "Are they celebrating or mourning the 36?"' Arun revealed.

It would be during this gathering that Rahane would address the group for the first time as a leader, but only after Kohli had had his say.

As Bharat Arun revealed to us, this is the crux of what Ajinkya's message was that night. 'There is no point mourning. There are three matches to go, and there's no point going back into our shell. The whole world has given up on us. The cricketing fraternity, the former Australian cricketers are predicting that we'll get thrashed. People are writing negative headlines about us. People don't believe in our ability, but I strongly believe in us. It is just one innings, and we will show all these guys what we are capable of. For that we have to put the 36 all out behind us, and I'm sure we can surprise them.'

This was also the night when Shastri famously asked the team to wear '36 as a badge', so that it reminded them that things could never get worse.

The morning after the team dinner, the coaching staff decided to gather everyone for a meeting. The purpose was to have a bit of a brain dump of all their thoughts with regard to the batting and where it went wrong. The consensus was that the batters shouldn't allow the Australian bowlers to dictate terms to them constantly, like they'd been allowed to do in the second innings in Adelaide.

That was the mindset aspect of the issue. Now they had to turn to the actual technical side of finding ways to overcome the shock and awe of being rolled over as a team for so little. That led to another meeting, this time purely with the batters. Empowering them to think for themselves seemed to be the best idea.

'The good part was that we knew what to expect from Australia. They would hit that hard length and give nothing away. So, we asked the batsmen how we could be proactive—whether by taking a different guard or standing outside your crease or taking on the short ball—it was completely up to them. We asked them to think about it and practise it ahead of the MCG Test,' Arun revealed.

A decision was made to 'trial' a few solutions during a practice session on what would have been the fifth day of the Test. However, we heard morning showers prevented the team from having a hit-out. The following day involved travelling to Melbourne, which meant the batters had to wait another twenty-four hours before donning the pads again.

'Ravi told Puji and Co., "Tell me what is troubling you, or let's replicate what they are doing and try different things in practice before the second Test,"' said Arun.

From the first session at the MCG itself, it was evident that some players were definitely keen to try different options. Mayank Agarwal was the first batter in the nets, and Shastri wasted no time in getting in his ear. He, in fact, walked him to his batting end. The two then had a chat before India's senior opener got going. There were a couple of edges and a streaky inside edge within the first 7–8 balls that Agarwal faced, and Shastri was in there again, making a point. The sounds of 'Shottt, Mayank . . .' echoed around the MCG repeatedly over the subsequent half hour before it was time for batting coach Vikram Rathour to jump in with Agarwal.

At one stage, having moved to the adjacent net, the right-hander re-marked his guard, asking for middle (he'd stood at leg stump previously). And a bemused Shastri was quick to butt in, asking the opener, who'd made 17 and 9 in Adelaide without looking convincing, to not change things around to such an extent. Agarwal nodded back and spent the next twenty minutes switching between the different nets.

Pujara was seen changing his guard on numerous occasions. He also seemed to put a lot of effort into perfecting the leave. '*Ye wala theek tha na* (Was this one all right)?' he repeatedly asked Rathour as he shouldered arms. He also kept asking the batting consultant to try and get the ball to seam away from him after coming in from a slightly wide angle, like he was facing Josh Hazlewood. This was Pujara doing what all great batters do: trying to eliminate any chance of his getting out the way he did in the second innings of the Adelaide Test for no score.

On a brighter note, Jadeja rolled his arm for thirty-odd minutes and then padded up to face the Indian pacers for close to an hour. There was no doubting in our minds that if Jadeja was fit, he would be an automatic selection. The all-rounder didn't seem to be hampered in his movements.

In the midst of all the batters knocking away the bad memories of the previous week, Navdeep Saini and Mohammad Siraj were busy trying to impress captain Ajinkya Rahane with incisive spells in the far net. They were still in good rhythm when Pant walked in. Pant's appearance in the nets ahead of Saha was the first clue that perhaps India was thinking of tinkering with their line-up. The aggressive left-hander didn't seem to have any difficulty at all in dealing with the pacers and looked very positive against the spinners too, except while facing R. Ashwin, whom Pant showed a lot of respect to, even inquiring on a couple of occasions if the off-spinner felt he'd played him well. '*Theek khela na, bhaiya* (Did I play all right)?'

Shastri was the one who called an end to Pant's nets session, calling him over for a chat. Then, with his arm over the wicket-keeper's shoulder, the coach passed on some batting tips, ending the exchange with a very positive, '*Tu dekh, apne aap ho jaayega* (You'll see, it'll happen on its own).'

There was speculation about K.L. Rahul opening the batting, but he was nowhere to be seen in the early stages of training. Gill, in the meanwhile, was one of the first players in the nets and had to face the brand-new Kookaburra. The youngster played some splendid drives and looked secure against all the bowlers. After another of his firm punches down the ground off Siraj, Shastri walked over to him and said, 'Shot! You are ready, young man. *Chal, bas hogaya* (Okay, that's enough for you).'

'He was batting with such confidence. He was hitting the ball crisply, and I could tell he was in a good mindset. Last thing you want is for him to get a couple of good balls in the nets and create doubt. I wanted him to be in a positive mind frame, and he had a decent hit-out,' Shastri would say later.

As the session progressed, we observed Rahane and bowling coach Bharat Arun spending a lot of time with Siraj. It appeared like they were discussing exactly where to bowl and the different field placements. Shastri would later join the discussion. Two days before the match, we had a fair indication of the playing XI. The only doubt was whether Jadeja was fit.

On 24 December, two days before the Test, Jadeja was once again one of the first to bat in the nets. The all-rounder also had a light trundle before disappearing back into the dressing room. Gaurav decided to peek inside the stadium to see if there was a fitness test being conducted but returned with no joy.

Rahane and Pujara had a decent hit-out in which both batters were tested by Natarajan and Saini. Natarajan had been constantly in Arun's ear, picking up every valuable tip the coach had to offer. He would also accompany the bowling coach to the middle every time Arun would walk over during the intervals to inspect the pitch. He was forever under the learning tree and loving it. One thing he seemed to grasp quickly was to adjust his wrist to swing the ball back into the right-handers. For 20–25 minutes, Natarajan tested the edges of Pujara's as well as Rahane's bats. He would later bowl from around the wicket to imitate Mitchell Starc's angle, and also got a bit of reverse swing with an old ball.

Siraj's presence at the training session was more in the garb of a batter. The fast bowler from Hyderabad played some audacious strokes in the nets and even chirped back saying, '*Match mein bhi aaisa khelunga* (I will do it in the match as well).' He lived up to his words, too, by the way.

Those players who weren't in the nets area were in the middle of the MCG, getting tested through various fielding drills set up by R. Sridhar. As all the Indian players disappeared down the tunnel that links the MCG nets to the ground, we picked up our bags, still unsure on the status of Jadeja's fitness.

As we started to walk to a nearby café to grab some lunch, I told Gaurav, as the consummate professional that I can be at times, to wait for a few minutes and check if the team had left the ground. We took a few steps towards the grandstand only to notice a couple of India's physical conditioning coaches walking back out to the training area. They would be closely followed by Jadeja for what would be the 'fitness test'.

It wasn't an elaborate affair and mainly involved getting the all-rounder to put in some sprints up and down the pitch. Jadeja, usually the quickest between wickets in the Indian team, looked his rapid best and in no visible discomfort. The 7–8-minute session ended with his galloping back and forth for three virtual runs, all in the space of 8–9 seconds.

At the end of it, he looked at us with a grin and said, '*Kitna bhagaaenge ye log* (How much will they make me run)?' He then departed the scene with a big smile on his face, while the two coaches seemed equally pleased with his performance. We'd got our answer: Jadeja was fit. Oh, there were also some haircare tips passed on to him when he informed me that he wanted to keep growing his lustrous mane. And as some sort of authority on the subject, I can assure you that when it comes to quality of hair, Jadeja is in the elite group of cricketers anywhere in the world.

Having more or less confirmed the playing XI for the match and been told that the Indian team was opting out of the optional training session on Christmas Day, we walked across into the city, past Yarra Park, to enjoy a hearty south Indian lunch at the famous Saravana Bhavan in the heart of Melbourne's city central.

★ ★ ★

It was a gorgeous morning in Melbourne for the start of the Test match. The Covid restrictions meant that the Boxing Day crowd capacity was reduced to only 30,000 spectators. The pitch was supposed to be like the very good one we'd had for the New Zealand Test the previous summer, which meant it would have something for the bowlers in the first session. The curator Matt Page had left 11 mm of grass on it, but it was well rolled.

Noticing local lad James Pattinson sussing out the pitch, Bumrah made a conscious effort to walk over to his then Mumbai Indians teammate for a long chat. Given that it was a cloudless day and based on what the experts were saying, it seemed inevitable that the captain who won the toss would bat.

There was a lot of energy about the Indian team in the huddle. And also a lot of emotions when Ashwin handed Siraj his cap. Holding it in his hand, the fast bowler held back tears and looked towards the heavens before telling the group: '*Mere abbu ne mujhe yeh mauka diya he, aur iss mauke ka pura fayda uthaunga* (My father has given me this opportunity, and I will make the most of it).' All the players quickly mobbed Siraj and embraced him.

Unfortunately for India, they had no luck with the toss, and Tim Paine had no hesitation batting first. Rahane was slightly dejected walking back to the dressing room, as if he'd let the team down. As the skipper crossed paths with Shastri in the players' tunnel, the head coach had a few wise words for him: 'Don't worry, the pitch is slightly damp, and it might work in our favour. Just keep all your bowling options open. Based on my experiences of the MCG pitch, if it has moisture, then it could turn.'

The Indian coach recalled having taken two wickets in the first session of the Test match at the MCG in 1985 and felt the pitch could behave similarly.

He was right. While Bumrah and Yadav bowled a tight opening spell, the commentators made a note of the moisture in the surface, as did Rahane. At the conclusion of Bumrah's fourth over, the Indian captain ran from gully to have a quick chat with Ashwin at mid-off.

Two over later, the eleventh of the innings, the wily off spinner was on to bowl from the Members' End. Ashwin struck twice before the lunch break, and could have easily had a third, to give India an upper hand. Rahane's decision to bring on a spinner proved to be a masterstroke and a pivotal moment in the series.

'Bumrah and Umesh had bowled splendidly with the new ball. I knew the Australians would be looking to attack, especially if Siraj, a debutant, came on to bowl. So I thought, given the wicket was damp, why not bowl Ashwin. He'd bowled so well in Adelaide, his confidence was up. I just wanted to check he was ready for it—which he was,' Rahane would say later.

You wonder, though, how many Indian captains would have still taken a punt on their premier spinner this early on the morning of a Test at the MCG. This was where Rahane's style of leadership shone through as he let Ashwin not only set his own fields but also control the momentum of the game.

Ashwin was also allowed to persist with the field formations he had in place, even if it meant having only two men in front of square on the off side, despite Marnus Labuschagne's persistence in making room and trying to force the spinner through that gap. Or having the leg gully a few inches to the right of a traditional backward short leg to Tim Paine. You could sense that the freedom to be himself had added a spring in Ashwin's stride. To the extent that, at one point, he convinced Rahane to give him an extra over, even after the captain had got Umesh Yadav to loosen up and take his cap off. It became apparent that under Rahane, the players were trying to be the best versions of themselves rather than live up to his idea of their respective best versions.

It was midway through the day that we realized the importance of the conversation between Ashwin and the two senior coaches at Blacktown Oval.

India was on top at lunch, but the coaching staff knew the real test would come in the afternoon session once the moisture had dried out and the ball had got old. This was where the 'leg-side' theory was to become prominent, and debutant Siraj had a key role to play. The youngster had not sent down a ball in the first session and was slightly despondent during the break.

'He came in at lunchtime and said, "Sir, *bowling hi nahi mill raha hai* (I'm not even getting to bowl)." You will get a bowl.

When you get a bowl, just think about bowling on one spot and about the strategy we've discussed. Maybe when you have gone through what he had, your ability to focus or concentrate is a lot more, and that is what he did, because the way he bowled was superb,' Arun told us.

Siraj was introduced into the attack in the first over of the second session. It took him a spell to overcome the nerves, but after that he followed on the good work of Bumrah and Ashwin. He would improve with every spell from that point on for the remainder of the series. His ability to hit the seam and be consistent meant that Rahane had the freedom to keep attacking from his end, which worked as Siraj knocked out two massive middle-order wickets in his nine-over spell, which sent Australia deeper into the mire.

It would be the wicket of Labuschagne that would be etched in Siraj's memory forever. He leapt for joy and pointed to the sky. The ball before, Rahane had asked Gill to move five yards finer at leg gully, and ten seconds later, the Australian No. 3 flicked the incoming ball straight to the man.

One of the commentators on air described it as an 'unlucky' dismissal. But in their dressing room, the Indian think tank felt a sense of satisfaction. In their minds this was not a fluke. This was all part of a well-thought-out plan that was devised almost four months earlier.

Clearly, the Indians had arrived at the MCG with very specific plans for the Aussies and executed them cerebrally. But it was also one of those days where, often, the bowlers were seen captaining themselves—the responsibility being shared among Bumrah, Ashwin and Ravindra Jadeja.

The impetus and constant positive reinforcement came, of course, from the new captain. He had been stereotyped throughout his career as being a cricketer who's forever inhibited by his own supposed insecurities, but this Boxing Day was all about Rahane breaking free and showing what he really is made of.

He never took a step back as the leader of the hungry pack who'd smelt blood and then went for the kill when the Aussie tail came around—not letting them wag and be a nuisance, as had been the case so often in the past. From letting Siraj lead the team off after the tea break to repeatedly being by his bowlers' side when they occasionally didn't get it right, Rahane was there for his players when and where it mattered, without ever dominating the frame for too long.

It was an impressive showing with the ball, but nobody displayed India's no-holds-barred approach at the MCG better than Shubman Gill. He started by surviving one of the most challenging nine-ball spells we've seen a debutant having to endure at the start of his career. There was also a seminal moment during this first foray of his, when Gill stepped out to Lyon and smashed him past mid-off for a boundary. The stroke was as significant as Lyon's reaction—the off spinner turned immediately as the ball went past the fielder and stared at the debutant as if to say, 'Who the hell are you again?'

There were countless number of times when the ball just beat the bat. As one of the coaching staff would point out, 'There were more play-and-misses in that brief evening session at the MCG than the whole of the second innings in Adelaide.' Maybe Shastri was right. Maybe God, or some sort of divine intervention, had occurred in the Australian dressing room on that fateful day in Adelaide.

★ ★ ★

Rahane had shown his game awareness and his ability to take control of the game without forcing the issue as the fielding captain on Boxing Day. Two days later, he was doing the same with bat in hand.

With Vihari for company, Rahane's strategy was to rebuild the innings, not just in terms of runs but also softening the ball up, to make sure that the influencers in the middle order, Rishabh Pant and Ravindra Jadeja, were playing when batting conditions were at their best.

After watching the Australian pacers slice through the Indian batting in Adelaide, the coaching staff wanted to devise a formula to upset the rhythm of Hazlewood and Cummins. One simple solution was to bring in the two left-handers in the middle order.

'In Adelaide, all our batsmen were right-handers. It meant Cummins and Hazlewood didn't have to alter their lines. With two left-handers, the balls that were good deliveries to right-handers in Adelaide were just simple shots off the hip for runs. It meant they had to change their lines, and in a way we were already upsetting their rhythm with our team changes,' explained Arun.

It would be the left-and-right-hand partnership between Jadeja and Rahane that would allow India to seize control of the Test after the second day's play. Both the batters picked the right moments to attack as well as defend for good measure.

Jadeja had walked to the crease when the lights had to be turned on. It was dark and gloomy. The temperature had started to drop rapidly, and even if the ball was sixty overs old, it had started to play a few tricks.

'The ball had got old, and our first instinct was to counterattack at that moment. But suddenly, it got cooler, and the ball started to jag around. So we had a chat and decided to bat normally for a while and then re-evaluate the situation,' the captain would say later.

Despite having a seventy-odd-over ball to contend with, the pair stayed reserved as they added just 38 runs in the eighteen overs after the tea interval. While the new ball was only a couple of overs away, Rahane was aware that two sessions on a muggy, overcast, humid day would eventually take their toll on the Australian bowlers. Instead of going back into his shell, he decided to attack the second new ball. The duo added 44 in ten overs, with Rahane doing the bulk of the scoring and in the process notching up his century.

'Rahane was just brilliant. He led from the front. He assessed the conditions so well. He attacked at the right time. It was probably the best innings he has ever played. People also underestimate the role of Jadeja in that Test as a batsman and a bowler. He proved why he was so crucial for us—a genuine all-rounder,' said Arun.

Jadeja's transformation as a Test batter, and therefore a more rounded bowler, started during the 2018 tour of England. The all-rounder had been dropped from India's T20I and ODI squads. Hardik Pandya was the premier all-rounder in the Test set-up, and Jadeja found it difficult to understand why he was on the outer. Unable to digest the thought, Jadeja decided to seek the two senior coaches for their opinion. Bharat Arun remembers this very clearly. He recalled, 'After the Lord's game [second Test], he came to me and said, "What is happening, paaji? They don't seem to be picking me?"'

It led to a few elaborate meetings between Jadeja and the two senior coaches, both together and separately. According to Arun: 'It started with me saying, "You are a terrific batter, but you need to get out of your shell with it. You need to learn how to bat with tailenders, because you come in at No. 7 or 8. If you bat with batters, then it's okay, but when there are bowlers to come—think about how you will bat."'

Arun went on to ask Jadeja to start working on different scenarios, especially when it came to batting with the lower order, which was vital as a No. 7. It involved the art of farming the strike while letting his partners build in confidence; but also, using his ball-striking skills to start scoring quicker.

Jadeja took all of Arun's recommendations on board. But he wanted to seek further clarification, so he decided to approach the head coach. Shastri not only echoed Arun's thoughts but went one step further by providing some technical advice.

'Ravi told him the same thing, but in his own style. "Now you have taken the initiative, come—look at your bowling. You are bowling from one spot, you don't utilize the crease or the angles, you don't bowl over or around the wicket—nothing. You constantly bowl from one spot, and people have figured that out. But you have ability to do all that. You are blessed with a beautiful action. You just need to create variation. You bring all those components into your bowling and also plan it all during the net sessions . . . Also, with your batting, when you go to the nets, imagine different scenarios. *Abhi thoda maarke khelunga* (I will now hit the ball), or I'm going play with a soft hand to run quick singles. Then all of that will come in handy to play with the tailenders.'" Arun revealed.

It was a defining conversation in Jadeja's career. He promised the coaches that he would apply all the advice during the practice sessions.

He then had another session with Arun, this time specifically about adding more depth to his bowling repertoire but also trying to get on top of his own game. 'I said, bowling from different angles is important, but what is more important is understanding what happens when you bowl around the wicket. How does the ball behave differently if you change the angle? You need to understand on your own. You can discuss all this with me at practice, but when you are in a game scenario, you need to realize and observe on your own.

'I said, whenever M.S. Dhoni used to tell you to bowl over the wicket, you would do it; if he said around the wicket, you would bowl around. Did you know why he was asking you to do it? He was telling you to do it, and you were doing it. You need to start thinking about it? What will happen? How do I fox a batsman, or how will he get foxed? If you understand all these aspects, you will take your bowling to another level.'

That both coaches were on the same page about where he stood as a Test cricketer, without having had to confer with each, other added to Jadeja's confidence. What added to his confidence even further was the fact that they were candid enough without beating around the bush with any 'coach talk'. No 'this is just a phase'. No 'you are still a good player, just stick to your processes'.

Jadeja is then learnt to have gone and thanked Arun for his honesty. There had been attempts to get the message through to Jadeja earlier too, but it was only then, with his future under some sort of a cloud, that the talented left-hander decided to embrace their philosophy.

The way he batted and bowled at The Oval in 2018 marked the beginning of Jadeja's transformation as a Test cricketer. The start of the period where he went from a handy batter to genuine all-rounder. His celebration after reaching the half-century there summed up the new Jadeja as he brushed off his bat, as if to say that despite not having been utilized for a while, the willow remained as potent as ever. He then pointed towards the Indian badge on his shirt and towards the Indian coaching staff.

After that match, he walked up to the coaching staff and said, 'Finally, I'm batting like an all-rounder, because you guys treated me like one.'

He was certainly batting like one at the MCG on Day Three. The fact that Mitchell Starc decided to give him a 'send-off' after dismissing the southpaw reflected the frustration his assured batting had inflicted on the Australian bowlers. His crucial innings of 57 had enabled India to gain a lead of 136.

The emphasis was back on the bowlers and Rahane the captain. The first twenty minutes was a quick glimpse of the series thus far in a nutshell, with Joe Burns failing again and India losing another bowler to injury. Umesh Yadav walked off holding his calf, which meant India would be without two of the three premier fast bowlers, Shami and Umesh, for the rest of the tour.

The loss of Umesh didn't stop India from deviating from their plans. Apart from getting the Indian bowlers to bowl a lot straighter, there was also a very fixed plan to starve Steve Smith in particular of boundaries—to not just check his run-scoring flow but to put the lid on it.

'We didn't want to give Smith any boundaries. Our main mantra was if Smith was going to get a hundred, let him take 250 balls. The line we decided to bowl and the fields we set. If he was going to make a ton—hats off to him,' said Arun.

Smith's major concern this series was Ashwin. Twice in two innings, he'd got the better of him. And you could see how much of an impact Ashwin had had on Smith when you saw the premier batter shadow-practising for the off spinner while at the non-striker's end, with Bumrah running in.

To add to the significance of the moment, Ashwin was right in front of him, observing this from mid-off. So, no wonder that Smith found a new way of getting out to another bowler, Bumrah this time. India, Ashwin in particular, had just got into his head. And what Smith was attempting to do when he was dismissed was come right across his stumps to try and play the ball finer to avoid the two square legs.

'I was close to Smith when he was walking back, and I cannot repeat what he was saying [to himself], but I can tell you our tactic had got into head,' one of the Indian players would later tell us.

The battle between Ashwin and Labuschagne was equally intriguing. Rather than come straight at the ball and look to play it with the turn, Labuschagne preferred to stay back, make room and hit Ashwin through the off side. By not having a cover fielder in place for long periods, Ashwin kept tempting him to continue doing that. But he rarely bowled him the one that went straight on with the angle. Instead, he changed his angle of attack, went around the wicket, and still let Labuschagne get back and push against the spin.

Having got the right-hander into the mindset of playing at everything, Ashwin picked the right moment to test him with a floater before bowling a delivery that drifted away in the air and, upon landing, kept going that way. The dip on it also meant Labuschagne was beaten on length, and the result was a catch to Rahane.

Both Gaurav and I had thought then, and still do, that Ashwin had set up Labuschagne in a brilliant way, and the ball that eventually dismissed the Australian No. 3 was by far the ball of the series. Siraj and Jadeja nabbed a couple of wickets between them as India finished Day Three well in a commanding position.

'There were no nerves as such. We just reinforced our plans in the morning huddle. We knew Cummins could bat, and Green was well set, so we ensured that all the hard work was done. Let's not relax,' a senior player told us later.

Green batted with determination, and it would take a terrific reflex catch by Jadeja to end his valiant innings. So quick was Jadeja to grab the ball that it took poor Green some time to realize that he'd been caught. After the fall of another Australian wicket, a senior player was left flummoxed by the words of an ecstatic Shubman Gill on debut:

'*Jaldi khatam karo, bhai log. Kyuki main aake match lunch ke pehele hi khatam kar dunga* (Let's finish this early, so I can come out and hit the winning runs before lunch), so we can enjoy a victory lunch.'

It would take an hour after the lunch break for India to register the victory, but Gill had lived up to his words by stroking a breezy 35 off 36 balls. The entire Indian contingent, including all the coaches and reserve players, made a conscious effort to be on the boundary line as India closed in on a remarkable win. Aptly, it would be Rahane who would hit the winning runs.

'Chasing small targets, you can get nervous. But the reality is, if you strike a couple of good blows, then it deflates the opposition really quickly. When I walked out, I just decided to remain positive, rather than thinking about the small target. In my first Test as captain, we had to chase a similar sort of target, and I hit a couple of boundaries on the first few balls, and the game was basically done. I did the same in Melbourne,' Rahane would say later.

The celebrations on the field were rather muted. This was, after all, one of India's greatest wins ever. They came here after having lost their captain, their serial wicket-taker and, to an extent, their dignity, following the 36-all-out debacle. Then they lost the toss on what looked like a Boxing Day designed for batting.

But there were no wild celebrations. There was no mad rush of players on to the field. There was no uprooting of the stumps.

There were no bear hugs or anyone jumping on anyone. The Indians could have justifiably indulged in any of this, if not all.

Rahane quietly hugged Gill before shaking hands with all the Australian players. All the players embraced each other, and their glowing smiles slowly disappeared down the tunnel into the dressing room.

To our surprise, it was Shastri who fronted up to the media after the win. We had expected Rahane, given that not only was he the captain but also the player of the match—the first-ever winner of the prestigious Jonny Mullagh medal, to be precise. The coach did get criticized in some quarters, with some alleging that he was trying to steal his captain's thunder.

We would later learn, however, that Rahane was mentally exhausted and filled with too many emotions. Shastri had recognized how much it meant to him to be with the team after the win. And it was only after he'd asked Rahane about what he would prefer that he stepped up to do it.

As was the case before the game, Siraj had, understandably, broken down, and Rahane wanted to stay by his debutant's side.

'We also raised a toast to Siraj. It was his debut, and at the end he couldn't hold it in. He just broke down, and Ajinkya had to walk up and give him a big hug. Ajinkya said, "Let it out, we are your family here,"' according to one of the players who was present there.

India's feat in Melbourne also proved that there was no one way of winning in Australia. That a visiting team doesn't need to really take the game to the Aussies or try to beat them at their own game.

The familial feel was very apparent in the end as the Indians stayed back at the MCG, taking turns to walk out on to the iconic field and snap pictures and selfies for many hours after Rahane had scored the winning runs in what was one of India's greatest comeback wins ever.

10

Ravi Shastri, Champion of the Champions

'I was there last week,' he points to the floor next to him, 'licking the bottom.'

Dramatic pause.

Followed by a roar. 'Today, I'm here. On top of the world. The Jeeeee . . . the fucking EM SEE JEEEE . . . The Jeeeee! Can you believe it?'

It was the day after India had pulled off a sensational victory in the second Test in Melbourne. Just over ten days since the embarrassment of Adelaide. Both Gaurav and I had been asked to come and join Ravi Shastri and Bharat Arun for lunch at a restaurant on the banks of the Yarra River. And yes, the head coach was very excited.

Shastri had experienced glory before at the MCG. He'd driven an Audi all around the vast expanses of the 'G for good measure. But this felt different. This felt a lot more special. It was the fight his team had shown. It was the character they had displayed. They'd recovered, after all, from one of the lowest points in Indian cricket history to so quickly create one of the greatest moments of all time.

The nature of the turnaround from Adelaide to Melbourne was such that even Shastri and Arun were only now beginning to fathom what Ajinkya Rahane's team had pulled off at the famed venue. And in this state of joy, even Shastri, for once, wasn't able to find too many words to describe how he was feeling. 'The Jeeee, guys, the MCG, I can't believe where we were last week to where we are now and how proud I am of this team!'

He must have repeated it a few times too. You couldn't blame him, though. It really was that exciting to have been there at the MCG, to witness Rahane calmly guiding his team home on the fourth evening, against all odds.

Gaurav had reached before I had and had already heard this bit a few times. I had been out with my wife, Isha, who does accompany me quite often to Melbourne for the Boxing Day Test. It was also the summer where she developed a very strong affinity for Test cricket—one of the many great feats achieved by the Indian team on that tour, you can say. But her keen interest didn't last beyond that summer. As it turned out, we were together when the lunch invite came through, and since she anyway wanted to say goodbye to Gaurav, I asked her to join us, even if only briefly.

Her stay ended up being slightly longer than brief. That was because she hit it off right away with both of India's senior coaches. And the virtue that all three seemed to bond over was 'empathy'— they agreed that it was needed in large quantities in their respective professions. Isha was the one who brought it up, after having listened to the duo reveal their coaching philosophy and how it was centred around player welfare. As a special-needs teacher for over a decade herself, she immediately managed to connect with that sentiment and began connecting the protective attitude of Shastri and Arun towards their dressing room to how she is with her students in class.

In a way, it was her arrival that really broke the ice that afternoon. Shastri and Arun overwhelmingly accepted Isha's suggestion that they were, if anything, 'teachers' in their own right. And though she left soon, after having received a number of thumbs-ups from Shastri for some of the points she made, her brainstorming with the two had got them to start reflecting on their own respective approaches to leading a bunch of highly skilled athletes at the highest level.

'Empathy and empowerment,' Arun would point out soon after as being the cornerstones of their coaching philosophy. It made sense. Having seen the two operate from close quarters for a good 3–4 years, Gaurav and I had noticed both these values coming through a lot in their treatment and training of the players. In the environment they tried to create, where players were made to feel protected from any external negative influences and empowered to become better cricketers and people. Even if that meant Shastri and Arun had to put up barricades to block out the outside noise or become the barricades themselves. As long as their players remained unscathed.

Shastri would often talk about how his being thick-skinned ensured that people creating memes about him or criticizing a statement he had made in the press have no impact on him. Also, if people outside spent more time criticizing him, they wouldn't have much time left to go after his players. 'Let them make fun of the way I look or the way I walk. As if that bothers me. I know what your job is, and I respect that. Similarly, I also have a job as a head coach. It is to ensure I create the best environment for my players, and that means blocking out all the outside noise. If that means I need to make a radical statement or back a certain player, then I will do it. As a head coach, I should be accountable, and I have never looked away from that.'

Shastri had once recalled an incident from the previous Australia tour, when many had questioned and debated why Ravindra Jadeja was left out of the Test match in Perth, and pointed out the head coach's alleged role in the ambiguity and confusion that ensued.

'There were all these stories and speculation as to why we didn't play Jadeja. You guys were coming up with some terrific stuff,' Shastri said with a chuckle before getting into what had really transpired from his perspective.

'Jadeja bowled a few overs during the practice match and, being a former left-arm spinner, it seemed like he was putting in all the effort, but the ball was not ripping through—it was like a balloon. That was when I first noticed it. He had taken an injection before departing for Australia, and had played a match, bowled fifty overs and taken wickets. I watched him bowl in Perth and asked what was happening. He said, "I'm bowling it as flat and fast, but it's just not the same. I'm getting a slight pain in my shoulder."

'Now, with him at 75 per cent, I could not risk him. This was Perth. So why not Kuldeep? We didn't think he was still ready to be the first-choice spinner back then. Also, this was Perth. Where was it that I was going to need a spinner? It was always in Sydney or Melbourne. You think I'm an idiot that I will throw all my eggs in one basket and play Jadeja at 80 per cent, and then risk him, knowing if Ashwin isn't fit and Jadeja is out, then we won't have a finger-spinning option for the tour?'

Whether or not Shastri did control the narrative for the media, as some accused him of doing, will always remain a debate. What is a fact though is that he tried his best to stay completely honest and forthright with his players at all times. In Adelaide, after the opening day of the 2018 series, Shastri had asked all the players to assemble in room No. 12 on the second morning. India had scored 250 in the first innings, thanks to Pujara's 123, but it was the top-order dismissals that had displeased the Indian coach. It prompted Shastri to ask the batters to hand over their 'driving licences'. He was referring to the fact that some of them had driven at balls far too casually and given their wicket away.

He would back it up with a stern message and a discussion about not wasting this unique opportunity to beat Australia in their backyard. After the chat, it was established by the playing group they had to get through the tough periods, especially when Pat Cummins was in operation. The message had struck the right chords. Shastri had chosen the right time to articulate his message in his own way. In the second innings of the match, when Cummins bowled an inspiring spell, India would grind through the phase, scoring 12 runs in nine overs before going on to post a score that paved the way for victory.

Similarly, on the 2018 tour of England, there was a lot of talk about why Pujara was left out of the first Test. Many experts felt it was because of Pujara's inability to score fast. This was back when his strike rate had become a national crisis.

Shastri didn't bother about the multiple debates that raged on, even if many painted him as the villain of the piece. Behind the scenes, he had cleared the air with Pujara and given him the reason for the omission. Observing Pujara in the nets—he was here after a poor county season with Yorkshire—Shastri had identified a technical blemish. The right-hander was staying too crouched, and his head, as a result, was going across the off stump, causing his bat to come down at a different angle. He had discussed the discrepancy with the assistance of the then batting coach, Sanjay Bangar, and told the premier batter that once the issue had been sorted, he would return to his No. 3 slot. Pujara had fixed the issue in seven days and was picked for the very next Test match. Not only was he back in the side, he was also batting fluently in the third Test, en route to a score of 82. Shastri would be in his ear right away, predicting that he would score four hundreds in the next six Tests. When Pujara made a hundred at the SCG in 2020, his fourth in seven tests, Shastri joked, 'Don't take things too seriously, Puji.'

On the same England tour, after India had lost the first two Tests, there was a lot of talk about India's imminent whitewashing. Deep down, though, Shastri knew that his team had missed a golden chance to win the opening Test. The conditions had been so favourable to England once they had won the toss in the second Test that it was always going to be difficult to win at Lord's.

Even at 2–0, the head coach was confident that his team wasn't out of it yet. On the eve of the third Test, he would tell a couple of journalists, 'Watch if we get 300 in our first innings. We will blow England away.' India scored 329 in the third Test and went on to win by 203 runs.

Then there was the man-management side of coaching, once again an area that called for empathy and empowerment. At one point in Mohammad Shami's career, when he just didn't seem to be doing anything right, Shastri had pulled him aside and had a stern word about his having to work on his fitness. Shami had fallen behind in his training programmes, with his yo-yo test scores dropping well below the expected standard. Shami was told in no uncertain terms that whatever happens off the field, the one unpardonable sin for a cricketer is to start taking his sport for granted. There is no way back from that. He was told that working on his body and getting fitter was the only way back to the top. It led to a dramatic transformation as Shami spent the next three weeks working his backside off in the gym and also on his diet. The end result was shocking. The fast bowler had gone from 15.1 in the yo-yo test to then clocking 18.3. And Shami has never looked back since.

It also helped that developing an army of fast bowlers capable of winning Test matches overseas was the mantra that the Kohli–Shastri era was built upon.

It all started with that Adelaide Test in 2014, when Kohli stood in as captain for M.S. Dhoni. Bharat Arun recalls how Shastri had laid down the brand of cricket he wanted the team to play on that tour, and how Kohli had been very much on the same page: 'That was the trendsetting tour. Much before we embarked on that tour, Ravi had told the team that I don't mind if you lose 4–0, but the brand of cricket we play on this tour is going to determine what kind of cricketers we become. In Australia, you need to be aggressive, you cannot be docile. If you are, they'll eat you up. Give it back to them. So, we were not afraid of losing, and that you saw in the first Test match, where we nearly chased down 380 on the final day in Adelaide. We could have won in Brisbane, too. We made 400-odd, and they were 250 for six, and they won by four wickets. Then, after that, they put up 500-odd in the last two matches, and we still managed to draw them.'

'With Virat and Ravi came fearlessness. They instilled the concept that for us to win, we had to be prepared to lose,' said Arun. The empathy and empowerment weren't reserved only for the players; they were applicable to the support staff too.

'Ravi was fabulous with changing that mindset around. If Ravi believed in any of us as the support staff, then he would never look over our shoulder. He gave us complete freedom to have our own say. He never interfered with me or any of the other coaches we had during our time,' said Arun.

There were a lot of misconceptions about Ravi Shastri the coach. Whether it was about what he allegedly did after hours or what he didn't allegedly do during practice sessions. Those who were around the team or covering it at close quarters would tell you that Shastri was always the first man to walk in for a practice session and invariably the last to leave. And what Shastri enjoyed doing more than anything else after a day's play was to talk cricket or stories from cricket. Not only had he been involved in cricket from every angle possible for over forty years, he also possessed the inherent gift of noticing and remembering the smallest of incidents or statistics, whether it was from when he was a coach, player or commentator.

After the win in Melbourne, Shastri kept reminding the batters how creditable it was to score runs against Cummins & Co., pointing out that this was only the second time in the history of Test cricket that a team had four bowlers each of whom had taken more than 150 wickets.

During the series, in an interview with a Brisbane radio station, Gaurav had compared Shastri's coaching style to that of the legendary rugby coach Wayne Bennett. Gaurav was then surprised to find out that not only had Shastri heard of Bennett but had even met the renowned rugby coach during his visits to Australia.

The holistic view he'd cultivated over the years about the game also allowed him to spot the slightest of indiscretions or drop in focus of his players. It was the reason he would want to walk along the boundary or be almost groundside right after the lunch and tea intervals.

Shastri's logic was that it is in that period, right after the resumption of play, that a player's concentration is not at its peak.

He had always felt that this was the time to watch and observe each individual carefully. Not to forget that those first 15–20 minutes of a session often dictate where the rest of it is going. So if you ever noticed him walking around by the dugout or the boundary, he was doing so to ensure that nobody was being even slightly lackadaisical in that initial period. Seeing the coach at the boundary was almost like a wake-up call, if anyone did need one on the field.

And then there was always the technical side of coaching, which Shastri had a knack for and enjoyed the most—whether it was giving a few pointers to a spinner about his action or proposing a solution for a batter to help him overcome a strategy.

After all, it was Shastri who advised Kohli to bat outside the crease during the 2014–15 series down under. Shastri's logic was that since Kohli was an excellent puller of the ball, the Aussies would try to bowl a yard fuller, and he could cash in by being closer to the ball. As it turned out, Kohli went on to score four hundreds in that series.

On India's tour of New Zealand in 2020, Prithvi Shaw got a lot of flak after the first Test. Shaw had looked slightly out of sorts, registering scores of 16 and 14. There were three days between the first and second Tests. There was criticism fired from all directions, and all the experts wanted Shaw to be dropped.

However, Shastri was confident that all he needed was just one session with Shaw to help him overcome his shortcomings against the moving ball. A day before the match in Christchurch, Shastri stood outside the nets, in line with the crease, and simply talked to Shaw about his head position and transfer of weight for twenty minutes. That was all he needed and all that Shaw required. On the first morning of the Test on a green seaming deck at Hagley Oval, Shaw made a splendid 54.

Then there was his simple advice to Rishabh Pant before the Sydney Test in 2019. Shastri had noticed that Pant's approach of advancing down the pitch to Lyon had become predictable, so he challenged him to play the off spinner on the back foot a lot more.

He knew Pant had the skills to apply it, and the slower surface in Sydney would actually provide the keeper–batter with more scoring opportunities by going deeper in the crease. Pant took the advice on board and went on to score 159 not out.

Unlike most modern coaches, Shastri never gave throwdowns, but delegation was another of his great strengths. He would constantly be in throwdown specialist Raghu's ear, telling him to bounce the batter at the other end. If the batter was good enough to handle the short ball, Shastri would often go, '*Aur zor se daal* (Chuck it faster).' If Raghu got the better of the batsman, Shastri would yell from the non-striker's end, 'Too quick for you, na?' It was Shastri's way of getting his player going and performing not just up to his own standard but above it.

During the net sessions, Shastri had his eye on everyone. It didn't matter if you were an in-form opening batter, an out-of-form premier batter or a youngster trying to find your bearings. After Shaw's dual failures in Adelaide on this Australia tour, he made sure that the batting coach, Vikram Rathour, spent plenty of time fine-tuning Shaw's technique, armed with an iPad which was used to record every ball; he then walked over to Shaw asking if he felt comfortable.

In Melbourne, Shastri would be deeply involved with Agarwal. '*Off stump nahi dikh raha hai* (I can't notice your off stump),' he declared with delight in his voice at one point as Agarwal shouldered arms to a ball outside off stump. The head coach was also waiting for Agarwal as he finished his umpteenth net session. The two then spoke about the positions the opener was getting into. It looked like Shastri was getting Agarwal to limit his trigger movements by a bit, to make sure he was getting into the correct position quicker and also not playing the ball while on the move. At one point, he yelled, '*Ab sochna bandh, khelna shuru* (Stop thinking, it's time to start playing).'

As Shastri would often highlight, you simply couldn't focus only on the guys who are in the playing XI; your eyes needed to be on the entire squad. Bad habits can creep in anytime, and it was his job to ensure that the players had a good mindset.

Those who played under Shastri in the Mumbai Ranji trophy team would often say he was their favourite captain, because he would just inspire you with the way he was. You knew what you were getting with him. There were no half measures and always complete clarity with the messaging. There was also the feeling of being protected while he was in charge, that he would stand up for you against anyone who wasn't a part of the crew. He also had the ability to instil belief in players, to achieve the goals that at times even they themselves hadn't thought of. If he saw something that he believed could be made possible for someone, he would go out of his way to persuade that person to see it through his eyes. Like getting Rohit Sharma to open the batting in red-ball cricket or getting Jasprit Bumrah into Test cricket.

The Bumrah story is a fascinating one, since it gives you an insight into both the coach and the fast bowler.

Arun recalled how Shastri truly believed Bumrah was capable of playing the long format of the game. And in October 2017, Shastri decided to get Arun on board with this idea.

Arun said, 'We had seen him in the ODI match against Sri Lanka and thought he could do well in Tests. Ravi had talked to Virat about taking Boom to South Africa. Virat's big concern was his stamina. We spoke to his Ranji Trophy coaches, and he had bowled a lot of overs at that level and had impressive figures. So now, we had the tick of approval that he could last the duration and be capable of bowling fifty overs in a Test.

'Now it was time for us to get him in. We were in a cab, and Ravi called him and said, "What do you think of Test cricket?" Jasprit was immediately on board and spoke about how he was always keen on proving himself in that format. Immediately, Ravi told him, "You are going to play Test cricket in South Africa." To which he replied, "Sir, that is the best news I have got." All we wanted him to do was train hard and be conditioned. We knew the bowling would take care of itself.'

How right they were.

Like with the press, Shastri was never shy of taking on anyone if at any point he felt that his players weren't being treated fairly. His first stance during the 2020–21 tour of Australia was very straightforward. 'No families, no tour,' he'd told CA categorically when doubts emerged over the feasibility of getting some of the players' wives and kids into the country. If Shastri gave you the word, he would stick by it, and he expected the same in return. Initially, the Indian team had been told after fourteen days of quarantine that they would have to adhere by the same rules as the common public. It was on this basis that he told the team, 'The first fourteen days will be tough, but it will get easier from there.'

But after fourteen days, when CA decided to create a soft bubble and tried to impose various other measures, it left Shastri displeased. As Bharat Arun recalls, when a member of CA tried to show Shastri a document which consisted of all the new rules, the Indian coach grabbed and tore the document and threw it away.

And when the players started to feel suffocated or were forced to feel like 'caged animals', to quote someone in the dressing room, it was Shastri again who said, 'I will make a statement, even if it means they come after me.' He did so by marching into the SCG without his mask on. But that was also a perfect glimpse into Ravi Shastri the man—you got what you saw. The man without a mask.

11

The Sydney Spirit

'Australia is a racist country, no?'

It's a question you hear very often from people back home if you're someone from the subcontinent living in Australia. At times, you know it's more a declaration that you are simply supposed to agree with. But I never have. It's never made sense to me. Surely, a bunch of ignorant bigots and idiots cannot be said to represent an entire country anywhere.

Have I been subjected to racism in my life? Of course I have. I've been called a terrorist. I've been asked if I carry a bomb in my bag. I always seem to be the one who gets stopped for an impromptu bag-check while entering a clothing store. Always the fellow who gets asked at least by three different people if I've paid for my medicines at a pharmacy. I've had some rather choice words yelled at me by strangers in moving cars while waiting to cross the road. I've had some rather choice barbs thrown to my face by those I know, at times in the guise of friendly banter. For the record, the term 'casual racism' is meaningless.

I'm surely not the first coloured person to have had to contend with any of this. And I surely haven't experienced this only in Australia. Racism is everywhere. I might even admit that perhaps I've had to deal with it the most where I grew up, in Mumbai, where nobody really batted an eye when I was constantly being referred to as a *kauwa* or crow.

So, I'd reached a point where I stopped acknowledging that clichéd jibe about Australia. Till it came to revisit me on 9 January 2021 in Sydney. Only this time it was from some Australians, who wanted to know if Australia is a 'racist country'.

My answer was still the same. But rather than dismiss it, like I would in the past, I chose to discuss the matter further. To even delve in deeper. All courtesy of a young man called Mohammad Siraj.

It was Day Four of the third Test in Sydney. Earlier, at 2.57 p.m. to be precise, Siraj had brought the action to a complete halt. He'd decided that enough was enough. And that he wasn't going to let the bunch of unruly fans behind him get away with what he insisted was 'racial abuse'. Incidentally, Siraj had moved to that fielding position by the boundary less than five minutes earlier.

I happened to be on commentary with SEN (Sports Entertainment Network) at that point. And I remember mentioning how it was the first time that Siraj had moved across to the Randwick end, basically the same spot where he'd been targeted the previous evening.

'That says a lot about Mohammad Siraj and his character. It must take a lot of courage for a youngster like him to return to that part of the ground. Classic Rahane, too, to have kept him away for so long,' I remember saying before literally letting out a loud gasp on air as we noticed Siraj walking towards the pitch just as Jasprit Bumrah was about to start running in to bowl. 'Surely not. Surely not again. Please tell me he's not been abused again,' I began screaming into my headset. Unfortunately, it was exactly what we feared.

What must it have felt like to be Siraj on the fine-leg boundary that afternoon? Here was a young man far away from home, on his first major tour with his national team, still grieving the death of his father, whose funeral he couldn't attend, being victimized through no fault of his own. If anything, he was doing exactly what those who went after him had paid to see him do, entertaining them.

Playing in only his second Test, Siraj had run in at full tilt like his life depended on it, ball after ball, and had created quite an impression on his teammates as well as on the opposition. Only to be brought down by a bunch of good-for-nothings having too much fun at the expense of someone else.

Later in the day, R. Ashwin would sum up the feeling of being on the receiving end of crowd abuse very succinctly: 'I had no clue about racial abuse and how you can be made to feel small in front of so many people. And the people actually laugh at you when you get abused. When you stood at the boundary line, you wanted to stand another ten yards in to keep yourself away from these things.'

That being 'made to feel small' is the bit that stays with you the longest when you've had to deal with abuse. That someone else was able to belittle you, and take joy in doing so, without your being able to stand up for yourself is what rankles the most. And that's what I tried to put into perspective when my fellow commentators very kindly let me have my say while we waited for the cops to intervene and for play to restart.

Tim Paine deserves a lot of credit for the way he dealt with the unfortunate incident. He was in the middle at that point, watching Cameron Green teeing off with some big sixes. And it was wonderful to see him walk all the way up to Rahane and Siraj and let them know that they shouldn't have had to be in this position. In the following months, Paine would talk about how bad he'd felt for the young Hyderabad fast bowler.

I was also very grateful to SEN for literally giving me free rein during the tea break, which began soon after the incident, to express exactly how I was feeling. And I will confess to have become quite emotional as I laid out the number of times I had been made to feel the same way as Siraj was. I then apologized for not having stood up like he had, for having turned to humour on too many occasions as my coping mechanism and perhaps inadvertently trivialized the impact of racism for others.

'You're taken aback at first. Then you kind of get used to it. But it doesn't make it right. You see if the racist comment comes from ignorance or from spite. You try and educate if it's the first, but you aren't sure what to do if it's not,' was the crux of what I said.

As the day wore on, the cricket in some ways took a back seat, at least till the time I spotted Rishabh Pant walking towards the SCG practice area for a nets session that would change the series for good (more on this in the next chapter). It became a day rather for self-reflection and introspection. Not just for me but for everyone present at the SCG and those watching it on television.

Both Gaurav and I were asked to go on various radio and TV shows to share our views on the Siraj episode. It was fascinating to note how distinct yet similar our views were on racism in Australia. Fascinating, too, when you think about how one of us had moved here thirty years ago and the other had lived here for three years at that point.

Gaurav and I did have our say. But at some level it didn't matter. For, Siraj had spoken the loudest without really saying anything.

That evening, as I returned to my Airbnb, a cosy little apartment block in Potts Point where I'd spent nearly a month, I was still lost in my thoughts. And as I stood at the main door of the building, fumbling through my bag for the keys, chucking my earphones and water bottle to the side, I noticed a couple walking out. I was relieved, thinking that I wouldn't need the keys any more to walk in through the secured door. I stood there smiling. But they didn't let me through, with the man saying, 'Mate, Uber Eats guys have to wait outside.'

Instinctively, my reaction was to make light of their rudeness, and I said something like, 'I wonder why you'd think that.' Neither of them bothered to respond; they just walked off. As I finally found my keys and took the lift up to my flat, it dawned on me. The cricket could wait. My piece for the day had to be about Siraj being the hero we all should be in the face of discrimination.

What made the events of 9 January even worse was the fact that Siraj had originally complained about the crowd behaviour on the previous evening as well, at the close of play.

I observed through a pair of binoculars that he walked straight to some of the senior players, including captain Rahane, and was seen gesticulating towards the specific part of the ground at the Randwick End. The umpires and security officials got involved right away, and we could see some of them head towards a handful of fans still sitting where Siraj had pointed. The match referee and the Cricket Australia chief of security staff were by now in a meeting with the Indian team management. The most unfortunate takeaway from that evening's episode was hearing one of the senior Indian players say, 'It's in their blood to look down upon us.' While I didn't quite accept the generalization, it was a glimpse into how much this incident had hurt the Indians.

It also told Bharat Arun a lot about a man he'd groomed from a young age. 'We'd told the junior players that if you hear something that you are not comfortable with, then go tell the seniors in the side. But just to have that confidence to be able to walk over to the senior and actually do it! I thought it was quite bold of Siraj. Most youngsters playing in their second Test match would think this is all a part of it, I can't complain about such things to seniors or the captain or people will not take it seriously . . . Despite all that, he came out openly and mentioned it to Jinx and others, which had to be admired.'

It was also perhaps the first time on this tour that the Indian team felt like they were under siege.

* * *

It had been building up, though. Maybe not so much on the field but certainly off it. The incident involving Rohit Sharma and a bunch of players spotted having a meal at an indoor setting in Melbourne, thereby breaching the protocols set by Cricket Australia, was only the tipping point.

Exactly a year ago, an Indian cab driver had treated some touring Pakistani cricketers to a meal in Brisbane, which became the most heart-warming story of that summer. Here, an Indian fan had done the same for some India players, and they ended up being placed in isolation, with images of them inside the restaurant being flashed in local newspapers under some uncharitable headlines. If you didn't know already, the world had changed in those twelve months.

The incident had triggered a slew of strong responses from within the Indian dressing room. Many of them had begun to feel like this was Australia beginning to intentionally make life difficult for them, because of the reversal in the Boxing Day Test. Though these fears were largely unsubstantiated, they certainly came through in the messages coming out from the visitors' camp.

With Covid cases continuing to rise in Sydney, the bubble there was to be much stricter. The players were to be given no access to any space except the hotel and the SCG. They had to stay within the confines of the hotel. News also began trickling in about Queensland having turned the screws tighter on their handling of the pandemic, which could mean that in Brisbane, the players might not even be allowed to leave their rooms, at least certainly not their floor.

The Indians seemed to be having none of it. Their belief that the Aussies were intentionally making life difficult for them, though logical in nature, only added to the confusion around the remainder of the Test series. Allowing crowds into the SCG while asking players to stay confined to their hotel felt to some of them like being treated as 'animals in a zoo', said one team official.

'All we want is what we've wanted from the start. To be treated the way "normal Australians" are. We are prepared to follow any protocol that we have to, especially since we've been testing negative,' was one take on the matter. There was also annoyance over the way Rohit and the other four players, outed as 'bubble-breachers', were being portrayed in the media. The Indian camp's version of events was that the only reason for them to go indoors was to avoid getting wet in the rain.

Eventually, the Indians did board the charter to Sydney, on 4 January, and we learnt that the players and staff had been asked to abide by the rules with regard to not leaving the hotel. But question marks remained over Rahane & Co. heading to Brisbane for the fourth Test, especially if there was to be a 'hard lockdown' in place.

But Cricket Australia remained steadfast in their position that the series would go ahead without a hitch. According to one CA official, the Indian team were informed at one point in Sydney that the chartered flight to Brisbane would be leaving as per schedule the day after the third Test, 'with or without the Indian team'. And that it would be up to the Indians, then, to justify their actions to the rest of the cricket world.

Thankfully, Nick Hockley, then CA's interim CEO, made sure that the situation was brought under control before it went out of hand. And around the time Siraj was describing to the stadium security his version of events, Hockley was spotted having an impromptu meeting with the Indian team doctor, the head physio and the manager, not too far away from the dressing room. It obviously had to do with clearing the air over the fourth Test, and it was good to see it end with thumbs-up signs all around.

Day Three of the SCG Test is generally when the great Peter Lalor and Ben Horne, along with the SCG Trust, organize a media dinner. Most of my colleagues had packed up and started walking away from the press box by the time Hockley met with the Indian support staff. I thought it was only fair that they were made aware of the scenes being played out, with meetings all around, in the centre. Let's just say that the media dinner was a slightly distracted affair, with almost every journalist in the press box that evening attending with their laptops still out and in use.

★ ★ ★

There had been a great level of intrigue about Rohit Sharma being a part of the Australian tour from pretty much a month before India's arrival down under. He'd suffered a hamstring tear during the IPL in October 2020, and that immediately raised concerns over his availability for the tour. Less than ten days later, he didn't feature in any of the squads announced for Australia. But he continued playing for Mumbai Indians in the UAE, leading to a lot of wild speculation around the state of his injury.

The usual statements—'If he's fit for IPL, then why can't he be fit for his country?'—started doing the rounds. The lack of clarity from all parties concerned only added to the muddle. Then, with two days left before the team's departure, Rohit was added to the Test squad. But unlike the rest of his squad mates, he flew back home on 11 November, with some reports suggesting he had done so for 'personal reasons'.

Virat Kohli's press conference on the eve of the first ODI only added to the confusion, especially with him expressing his own lack of clarity over the matter. He spoke rather candidly about how the team management had received an email stating the opener's 'unavailability' for the tour, with a two-week rest and rehabilitation period recommended for him. But then, how did seeing Rohit play for Mumbai Indians give Kohli & Co. reason to believe that he'd be on the flight to Sydney with them?

'After that, the only other information officially we have received on mail is that he is in the NCA, and he's been assessed, and he'll be further assessed on 11 December. So, from the time that the selection meeting happened to the IPL finishing now, when this email came about his assessment at the NCA, there has been no information, there has been lack of clarity. We have been playing the waiting game on this issue for a while now, which is not ideal at all,' Kohli said.

Kohli wasn't done, though. He went on to express his surprise over why Rohit and Ishant Sharma weren't undergoing their recovery in Australia in the presence of the team physio, like Wriddhiman Saha was.

The uneasy air wasn't lost on the Australian media either. For at least a week, the Virat–Rohit relationship was brought up on every radio show I went on. Most times it was pretty direct, too. 'So, mate, Rohit and Virat, don't really get along, now do they?' I played most of them off with a straight bat, but there were times when I couldn't help but express my own confusion over the matter.

As it turned out, Rohit and Virat never crossed paths on the tour. So there was to be no real conclusion as to whether there was indeed any beef between them at all during that phase. Those close to Rohit never deterred from their opinion that he would make the trip, come what may, if he was fit to do so. In fact, one of the Australia-based coaches at the IPL even recalls having shook Rohit's hand after the IPL final against Delhi and being told, 'I'll see you in Australia soon, mate.'

And on 11 December, it was made official that the classy Mumbai batter was coming over and that he'd be ready to play in the third Test.

The next issue on hand was where he would land and quarantine. A two-bedroom apartment overlooking the city in Sydney was obviously the preferred choice over a cramped hotel room in Melbourne. And he was also provided with some indoor exercise equipment to continue with his rehab. Rohit came out of quarantine on the morning after India won in Melbourne and had flown over to join them that very night—much to the overwhelming delight of his teammates and Ravi Shastri, as seen in a clip posted by the BCCI media team.

In the wake of the multiple departures, K.L. Rahul and Umesh Yadav joined that list soon after the second Test, and Rohit's arrival was looked at as a massive silver lining. Not only because it meant India had another senior batter to call upon but also for the uniquely calming vibe he brings to a dressing room, or any room for that matter.

It also meant that Ajinkya Rahane now had someone he'd grown up playing cricket with and one of his closest and trusted friends to fall back on during and after the match. You could see

Rahane do that often during the SCG Test, where he'd let Rohit speak to the bowlers and even set fields for them. Bharat Arun, for one, wasn't too surprised with the more inclusive form of leadership on view from Rahane, by the fact that Rahane would want to lean on his Mumbai mate.

'Rohit is a deep thinker about the game. He wants to have a lot of information on his fingertips, like the bowler's mindset, what is the plan we have at the time—he would sit through the entire bowlers' meeting, with each and every bowler. He'd then come to me and go, "*Paaji, mujhe laga usne theek se nahi samjha* (I don't think he understood you fully). Let us just go and explain to him again and make sure he has got the message." That is his attention to detail,' Arun said.

There's also the casual air to Rohit that makes him very approachable for players, both senior and junior. Arun has always been impressed by Rohit's ability to motivate those around him, even if at times it meant having a go at them.

Arun continued: 'He will talk to the bowler nicely at first and then slip in, "B★★★★★★★★ if you do something different *tere ko aisa maarunga na* (I'll bash you up)." But he says it in such a firm but friendly manner that even the guy doesn't feel threatened. He'll then double check, asking the bowler to repeat whatever has been suggested to him. And then, as a passing note, chide him saying, "*Nahi toh khudh ka dimaag chalaega aur kuchh alag kar dega* (Or else you'll use your brain and end up doing something different)," to much laughter all around.

'He is intense but also exceptional at understanding a player's strengths and shortcomings. He has an uncanny knack of understanding personalities, which helps him in forming those bonds with the players. Also, there is a lot of reasoning about his captaincy, it is not just intuitional. There is a lot of reasoning behind each decision. He was always open with me, and if he wanted something done, he'd ask me to have a word with Ravi, saying, "*Aap bolenge toh mana nahi karenge* (If you tell him, he won't disagree).""

Rohit is also someone who doesn't suffer fools. But again, he is not someone who wants to take himself too seriously. I've experienced it first-hand too. As someone who has had a reputation of mimicking him for years now, I often get called up to 'do a Rohit' in his presence. It was always the gag whenever Ravi Shastri spotted the two of us in the same space. But while Rohit has never minded my doing it, there have been times he's expressed his deep displeasure, not so much with the idea of my mimicking him, but more when he felt that the execution wasn't up to the mark.

And there was certainly some spirit-lifting on show when we arrived at the MCG nets on 2 January for what was Rohit's first hit on the tour. He was straight into it, having a long chat with Rahane while the rest of the team indulged in an interesting piggyback warm-up routine.

His first hit was not his best. And he was troubled as much by the flies as he was by the trajectory of the new throwdown specialist Dayanand Garani. But even here you could see a steely determination in Rohit's eyes and in his demeanour. He had come here to prove a point.

All around him, though, there were batters being smashed on gloves and on the helmet, with the practice wickets at the MCG beginning to look worn out. Pujara was smashed on his right hand; this left him in extreme pain, and he had to get some treatment. It was an injury he would carry till the end of the tour. Prithvi Shaw was laid low by a nasty delivery that didn't rise, leading to some alarm in the Indian camp.

Rohit looked a lot more like himself once India had arrived at the SCG. He was middling the ball much better and was also looking less stressed with how it was coming off his bat. He was still getting Bharat Arun to watch his back foot post the trigger movement and Ravi Shastri to keep an eye on his backlift.

Rohit was also using this time to constantly encourage his bowlers, the younger ones in particular—getting Navdeep Saini to be more consistent with his lengths, cheering T. Natarajan on every time he got the new ball to shape in smartly. Only Mayank Agarwal spent more time than him at the nets—having five sessions in all—but it looked apparent that Rohit would come in as opener, twelve months after he'd officially taken over that role. It also meant that India would probably get its most elegant opening Test pair ever in Rohit Sharma and Shubman Gill.

Pujara was battling through the pain. It would end up becoming the theme of his tour from this point on. But he'd copped a blow to the same middle finger that he'd injured at the MCG—this time, thankfully, off Kuldeep Yadav's bowling. It was still sore enough to make him wince in pain. Both Rahane and Shastri kept checking on him repeatedly to know if their key No. 3 batter was comfortable to continue batting. So engrossed was Pujara in getting his finger right that, at one point, as I greeted him with a customary 'Sab theek hai (All good)?', he just smiled, like always, and began describing the extent of the pain and how he was fighting it. It was also another insight into the genuine niceness of Pujara.

There was also an added focus on fielding as India prepared for the Sydney Test. R. Sridhar, the fielding coach, had recognized the SCG as being a classic cricket ground that slopes towards the outfield, with the grass on the inner square much shorter. That would ensure that any ball that beat the infield would speed towards the boundary. So it was important that the fielders were mindful of cutting off angles within the virtual circle and making sure that they cut off as many boundaries as they could. The team management had also identified that this would well be the best batting pitch of the series and that it was imperative for the fielding to be of the highest order.

And who else but Ravindra Jadeja to cap it off with one of the most extraordinary run-outs witnessed in this part of the world. It happened on Day Two, with Steve Smith on 130 and looking well set for more. He seemed confident of completing a second run as he scurried back after having tucked the ball off his pads. In came Jadeja on a gallop from deep backward square leg, picking up the ball and, literally in the same motion, chucking it to hit bullseye with one stump to aim. If fielding in cricket ever needed an entry for it to get accepted as an art form, this was it.

I couldn't help but ask him the next morning about where this particular run-out ranked among the many special ones he'd pulled off over the years. '*Sabse best wala* (The best ever),' he said without even blinking.

★ ★ ★

It's unlikely that Steve Smith would rate this to have been among his best tons, but it was an important one for him and his team. He'd end up having a bit of a lean trot in terms of centuries post this one at the SCG. He'd also, however, come into the India series following a quiet summer before the pandemic. And it wouldn't be too harsh to say that he'd batted against Ashwin in the first two Tests with a bit of siege mentality. Ashwin doubtless had been at his tantalizing best both in Adelaide and Melbourne.

We hadn't seen the customary use of the feet from Smith in the first couple of matches, and his success against Australia's two key batters, Marnus Labuschagne included, had prompted a discussion in the Australian dressing room during the week-long gap before the third Test. They even brought in former Sri Lankan off spinner Suraj Randiv, who lives in Melbourne these days, to help with the preparations. Labuschagne had his own plans and, as he always managed to do uncannily, prepared so well for Ashwin that he was literally replicating his shots from the nets in the middle, in the same order too, like he'd foreseen the ace Indian spinner's ball-by-ball plan. I also chanced upon a lovely piece of advice from Nathan Lyon to the new opener Will Pucovski, who seemed to be fretting over the prospect of facing Ashwin. After multiple chats, Lyon held the ball up towards the prodigiously talented right-hander and said, 'Play the ball, not the bowler.'

One of the methods proposed by the coaching staff was to try and play Ashwin a lot straighter rather than flicking or tucking the ball towards the square-leg region, which is generally how Smith and Labuschagne like to milk runs off spin bowlers. With Ashwin generating a lot of overspin on the ball, the leg slip and backward short leg had been brought into play quite a bit.

Smith was also shown videos of his batting against Ashwin from the 2014–15 series, where he used his feet a lot to loft the ball straight over long on or long off. The premier batter then took that planning to the nets and began practising it like a man possessed. And he had Justin Langer there at the MCG nets pumping him up like this was an outtake from the *Rocky* movies.

'Warriorrr, warrior,' he'd scream every time Smith would advance down the pitch and smash the ball into the roof of the net. Langer would even introduce himself as 'Ashwin coming into the attack' before beginning to wang down some off breaks at him. Langer would then give himself a cheer every time he got Smith playing defensively, going, 'Well bowled, Ashwin.' The half-hour-long session was laced with screams of 'Yesss, the warrior's back!' and 'There you go warrior, that's what we're talking about!'

At one point, bizarrely, Langer even broke into a 'Sachinnn, Sachinnn' chant. A few minutes in, he had Smith hooked on the warrior reference too, to the extent that when the head coach slipped up and referred to Smith by his usual nickname, 'Smudge', Smith corrected him saying, 'I'm the warrior.'

The rather intense preparation paid off eventually, as Smith did use his feet a lot more to Ashwin and kept popping him over the top of his head for boundaries towards the straight field. A year and a half later, in an interview he gave me in Galle, Smith would admit that he had not been proactive enough in the first two Tests that summer. He also spoke about how he had managed to put a bit more pressure on Ashwin in Sydney. Either way, it was a fascinating battle between two of the best cricketers to have ever played the game. Perhaps it's safe to say that honours were even, though Ashwin might claim the scales were tipped slightly in his favour, having dismissed his arch-rival on three out of five occasions.

This was the first time in a long while that India had played against Australia with both Smith and David Warner in the playing XI. It would be remiss if I didn't accept some credit for having safeguarded Warner during his first hit in the nets back from the groin injury. It was in Melbourne on 2 January, the same day when many of the Indian batters were getting hit in one particularly rogue net. We'd also seen a couple of Aussies, Labuschagne included, being struck painful blows. The net eventually was abandoned. Warner had walked in with Sean Abbott, who was also returning from an injury, after the rest of the team had left, since Warner wasn't yet part of the bubble. And the first thing he did, oblivious to what had transpired earlier, was to walk into that same rogue net.

I was there at that point with my dear friend and colleague Melinda Farrell, who did fabulous work throughout the tour, apart from having me as the recurring guest on her YouTube channel. Quite aware that Warner might not pay heed to me, I asked Mel to slip in a warning to the left-hander about what he was about to get into. It took her two attempts to get through to him. Thankfully, he did hear us, and even though he did check with the team doctor, who'd been around earlier, Warner switched nets without facing a ball. And thus, we, in some way, saved Warner's summer. Or so we will claim forever.

The batting bit was only incidental. What Warner really was focused on was seeing how much his groin had healed. And it was obvious from that net session itself that he was far from his 100 per cent, but in true Warner fashion, he was ready to play for his country, even if it meant he was standing on one leg. Gaurav and I bumped into Warner walking around with his family in a park the morning of the day when the teams left for Sydney. And we couldn't get over how the actual 'warrior' of Australian cricket was hobbling while pushing the pram around.

The fact that he was out of shape was quite apparent during his handful of knocks in Sydney and Brisbane, where he did seem quite hindered in his movements. And even if he did eventually end up on the losing side, Warner deserves as many plaudits as Ashwin and Pujara for having sacrificed his body and embraced his pain for the sake of his country.

* * *

It might pale in comparison with what they had to play with a week later in Brisbane, but India had gone into the SCG Test with a very inexperienced fast-bowling attack. And it was telling that Jasprit Bumrah, playing only his sixteenth Test, was the one handing out the Test cap to debutant Navdeep Saini on the morning of the match. It was also a sign of Bumrah's standing and seniority within the group. In less than eighteen months, he would, of course, be captaining India in a Test match at Edgbaston.

Prophetically, Siraj too was beginning to come across as a leader on the field. Playing only his second Test, he was happily walking over to Saini—who was playing his first—between deliveries with constant pieces of advice and encouragement. And when he had the ball in hand, the guy bowling from the other end would invariably have to field the first delivery of the Siraj over without his cap on, since he wouldn't have got the time to go retrieve the cap from over the boundary rope due to Siraj's eagerness.

There were some worrying indicators about India's performance on the third day in Sydney, where they did show signs of unravelling and succumbing to Australia's relentless bowling attack. It was also a day where their batters were peppered with strikes to the body, with physio Nitin Patel beginning to take great strides towards winning the 'most valuable non-player award' that he so richly deserved.

If during the afternoon Patel was busy tending to Pant and Jadeja, who'd been hit on the arm and thumb respectively, it was Bumrah's abdomen that needed attention as the shadows lengthened.

India had come to Australia without Ishant Sharma and Bhuvaneshwar Kumar, and had lost Mohammed Shami and Umesh Yadav already before the third Test. Now, unbelievably, there were fears that Bumrah would follow suit. Not that he was prepared to go out without a fight. He kept waving off Patel every time the physio approached him near the fine-leg boundary or during the drinks break. But the more he kept clutching and stretching, the more anxious the dressing room got.

On Day Four, Bumrah stayed on, but India were without Jadeja's services with the ball, while Wriddhiman Saha was back with the gloves in place of Pant. The dressing room had already started to go from housing the who's who to the who's left. It would only get worse, much worse.

★ ★ ★

India were very much under siege when Ashwin joined Vihari in the middle. I had spotted the off spinner on multiple occasions during the first session of play on Day Five. I really thought Ashwin was simply being superstitious, especially during the wonderful Pujara–Pant partnership. And we will read a lot more about the rise of Pant, including the incredible net session he had late on Day Four, which really summed up the 'mind over body' nature of India's performance on this tour.

Not to forget Pujara and the grit he already displayed for nearly two sessions. He may not have got the runs he had two years earlier, but Pujara, if anything, had become an even more immovable object now. And as with Smith and Ashwin, he had got into Lyon's head too. So much so that every time Labuschagne would step out to smother the spin against him, Lyon would scream

'Pujaraaaaa' at his teammate. It finally took a special delivery from Josh Hazlewood to knock Pujara over, after Pant had perished for 97 in a failed attempt to clear the ropes.

During the lunch break, I saw that Ashwin was on the balcony by himself. He was still not making the most of the rather comfortable chairs on the SCG visiting team dressing room balcony. It was then that I realized that maybe something was indeed wrong. As we know now, he'd bowled thirteen overs on the trot through excruciating pain, with nothing more than pills to suppress it, on Day Four, and even managed to get Smith out again. He'd then needed his wife and kids to help him stand up the next morning, after having spent the night crawling and rolling on the floor.

And as Ashwin gingerly made his way out to the middle, he was greeted by someone who, amazingly, was much worse for wear than even him. Hanuma Vihari had torn his hamstring in such a horrid fashion that he could barely move, forget walk or run. What Ashwin and Vihari ended up doing for the next two and a bit more hours would end up attaining legendary status. It was Test cricket at its most primitive and raw state. A fight for survival against the best bowling attack in world cricket at that point. The next man in was Jadeja, who sat in the dressing room padded up and with his left glove on with heavy padding underneath to protect his broken thumb; he prepared to walk out and bat with one hand.

Cricket is littered with stories of cricketers taking the field wearing bandages over their heads and faces and various other parts of their bodies—except the fingers of course, since that would distract the batters' attention. But neither Ashwin nor Vihari had any bandages to show for their pain and agony. One couldn't bend. The other couldn't move. But they were showing enough heart to make up for those deficiencies, and their attempts to thwart the Australians were working.

It was a unique position for the Aussies to be in, too. Yes, we've seen batting teams look to dead-bat their way towards a draw. But rarely would a bowling team have come across a couple of batters who literally wouldn't budge. So it was only natural, at some level, that the fast bowlers briefly forgot about getting them out and started focusing more on knocking and prising them out. It meant more pain for Ashwin in particular as his body was used like a dart board by Hazlewood and Cummins. But he simply refused to budge, despite being left coughing and grimacing in pain repeatedly. Much like Pujara at the Gabba a week later, there were times when you felt a referee would have asked for the bout to be stopped and awarded the Aussies a technical knockout win. Cricket umpires, for good reason, don't have such powers. Rarely had a cricket pitch turned into an MMA ring to this extent.

Looking back, these sound like scenes from a movie. While there have already been a couple of documentaries made on this remarkable tour, I'd say the Ashwin–Vihari partnership deserves its own exclusive film. And there was some crude element of romance added to the equation too, with the two batters exchanging chest guards and sticking it under their shirts at the back at the end of each over, much to the Aussies' frustration. Ashwin still couldn't sit when they went in for the tea break. Vihari was putting not just his body but his career on the line with his show of courage. He was already ruled out of the next Test, and with no big score to show for his steadiness in this series, his efforts here just put his fearless attitude further into perspective.

'Vihari told him, "Come what may, I will not give my wicket away." That was when Ashwin walked up to him and said, "I will give you a stand." It was easier for Ahwin to play Lyon because he was able to stretch forward. Vihari couldn't stretch, and it was easier for him to play the fast bowlers. They took that decision by themselves,' Bharat Arun recalled. 'Ravi was upset because Vihari was batting so well when he injured his hamstring. We accepted the situation. Ravi told the physio, "If he can bat, let him bat." Vihari also had the same mindset: I can bat, I cannot run, but I want to draw this Test match, I want to give everything I have. The physio said that he could help him manage the pain with some medicines, but neither of them would be available for the next Test.'

The bowling coach described Ashwin as having been in a sort of special zone with bat in hand. The off spinner would later talk about how he had reached a point in his head where he didn't mind dying on the pitch for his country that day.

Arun said, 'After the game it took him thirty minutes to come out of that zone. He had been extremely consistent with the ball and produced probably his best overseas performance. He said, "Here lies an opportunity for me to show my grit in batting." He said later that he felt like a zombie for half hour after the game. That said so much about his commitment to the cause.'

The longer they stretched the partnership, the more annoyed the Aussies got. Gaurav was informed later that there was a kind of fungus growing along the square at the SCG, and that made the wicket really slow and ensured that it did not deteriorate to the extent everyone expected. Earlier that summer, some of the New South Wales players had observed this as well and complained to the ground staff, but due to Covid and the number of games being played there was nothing they could have done about it.

And there was nothing that Paine seemed to be able to do about Ashwin and Vihari's defiance either. He'd already had an off day behind the stumps, having missed two catches off Lyon's bowling and another one that slipped past his glove later in the innings. It was sad to see him struggle behind the stumps, especially for those of us who'd seen him spend hours working on his craft. And it began to affect his mind, too, as he began to lose his cool and had that verbal exchange with Ashwin, which included the invitation to the Gabba.

It was maybe a glimpse into how someone's defence could impact you a lot more than their offence. To Paine's credit, he did call for a press conference the next morning to apologize for his performance, both as captain and wicket keeper, on what was by far his worst day on a cricket field as an international cricketer.

At around 6.07 p.m. Sydney time, Jadeja finally took his gloves off in the dressing room. The Aussie bowlers had taken theirs off a while back but to no avail. Ashwin and Vihari had pulled off one of the greatest rearguard efforts in the history of the game. If Test match cricket was all about character, India had won this game already.

Ashwin and Vihari were finally offered a seat as they were interviewed by the BCCI media team later that evening. But rarely had a couple of heroes staggered off a cricket field slower than Ashwin and Vihari did that day as they somehow pulled and dragged their battered bodies off the SCG, with the entire stadium on its feet.

For all the supposed bad blood on the field, the end also witnessed two very classy moments: Ashwin picking up a stump and offering it to Steve Smith as a souvenir, only for the Australian batter to give it back to him; and Paine running all the way to Ashwin, patting him on the back, and the duo laughing off whatever had happened between them in the heat of the moment.

Ajinkya Rahane nailed it in the end during the post-match presentation when he spoke about how the magnitude of India's achievement might not sink in tonight or even tomorrow. But it certainly would maybe after the series or in two months' time. SCG 2021 was one of Indian cricket's greatest moments and will go down in cricketing history as such.

As the sun set over the SCG, it was Australia who suddenly looked to be under siege. The Indians could sense it too. As Arun would put it, you could see it on their faces as the teams exchanged handshakes. And they could hear some of the Aussie players blaming all the wrong things for their inability to see India off here. It was a sign that they were rattled.

'It felt like a win for us. We'd also got their fast bowlers to bowl a lot of overs. We had come back from 36 all out, won in Melbourne and now pulled off this remarkable draw. We were euphoric and almost felt like the pressure was off us going into Brisbane,' Arun said.

I got a call very late at night, but not late enough for me to have finished my piece, from one of the head coaches. The euphoria was notable in his voice. You'd have thought that they'd already won the series. In some ways they had. The phone got passed around the room, and the other coaches chimed in with their own expressions of delirious joy. The consensus was that if this wasn't the greatest Indian team ever, it certainly was the toughest Indian team of all time. You simply couldn't help but agree.

12

Bharat Arun and the
Fast-Bowling Revolution

'Bhaaaat, do you want to be the bowling coach of India?'

'*Kya baat kar raha hai tu* (What are you talking about)?'

'I'm in England. I can't speak a lot, but just tell me. Are you interested in coaching India?'

'*Aisa mauka kaun chhodega* (Who would let an opportunity like this go by)? If you call me there now, I will drop everything and come. But for now, just hold on, I'm driving.'

'Fucking stop the car and talk to be me.'

It was August 2014. The man on the other end was Ravi Shastri. He had just been appointed as the director of the Indian men's cricket team. Bharat Arun was the first person he called. As Arun pulled over to the side of the road, he was given a brief rundown by Shastri: 'Look, I'm taking over in a few days' time. You can be the bowling coach, and can you do fielding as well?'

Arun said that at that elite level, the team needed another person for fielding. 'We have a very good coach in the NCA. He was with me at the Under-19 World Cup and on the A tour. His name is R. Sridhar. He is more than capable and has all the credentials,' Arun told Shastri.

'Sridhar?' came the reply.

Arun told Shastri that Sridhar played first-class cricket. 'But like me, he has been in the NCA for a while and has worked with a lot of the players on the A tour. He is a very good coach. He is also with Kings XI Punjab in the IPL.' Luckily, Kings XI had qualified for the IPL final that season, so that helped.

Arun told me: 'I recall it was a Tuesday, and the next thing Ravi said was, "I want you to be in England on Friday." At the time, I didn't have a UK visa or a flight ticket. He said, "*Uska tension matt le, woh sab ho jayega* [Don't worry about that, I will get that sorted]." That was exactly how it came to pass, and by Friday evening I was in London. I was officially the new bowling coach for India.'

★ ★ ★

As India embarked on the tour of Sri Lanka in 2017, one of the first questions Shastri was asked at the press conference was why Bharat Arun had been chosen as India's bowling coach?

Shastri defended the appointment of his former teammate and old friend saying, 'There's a track record. Fifteen years of his life have been coaching. It's outstanding, right from junior level to A teams to Indian junior World Cup teams, he's been a part of it. He knows these boys better than I do, because he's been in the system for the last fifteen years,' the head coach had said at the start of his new tenure.

During his playing days, Arun had never envisaged that he would take up coaching. He had represented India in two Tests and four ODIs. He also had quite the reputation for Tamil Nadu as a hard-hitting all-rounder and played in forty-eight first-class matches.

Those who witnessed Arun's maiden Test wicket, that of Aravinda De Silva, still regard it as one of best outswingers to be bowled in India. 'Pitched middle, hit off on the flattest of decks in Kanpur,' Shastri had once said. The Chepauk regulars who saw him play in the 1980s also claim that the biggest six on the iconic ground had come off Arun's bat.

Unfortunately, ongoing knee problems had forced Arun to retire at the age of thirty. Despite calling it quits at first-class level, he would still spend a lot of time at the Chemplast Cricket Club in Chennai, nurturing some of the young bowlers coming through.

'I had donned the role of a coach, but I was not qualified. Youngsters such as (Laxmipathy) Balaji were coming through, and they would pick my brains, and I would try my best to provide them with a solution or give them advice.'

Right from his younger days, Arun thrived on his curiosity about everything, starting with the universe itself. 'When we were kids and used to sleep on the terrace, I would often stare into the night sky and wonder what existed out there.' Perhaps it was this curious mind that inadvertently made him turn to coaching and what led to his rapid rise through the coaching ranks.

'From the technical side, I had never completed a course. So, I inquired formally, but there were no formal coaching courses in India, and you would have to do level two and three in Australia.'

Luckily, in 2000, the BCCI decided to conduct a level-two coaching seminar. Close to eighty former cricketers, including legends such as Bishan Singh Bedi, attended the informal coaching tutorial. It was during this gathering that Arun's thirst for coaching started to develop. He was soon appointed as the Ranji Trophy coach for Tamil Nadu and in a year's time passed his level-three coaching with a distinction.

The late Frank Tyson, the former England fast bowler who conducted all the level-three classes, recommended Arun's name for teaching the level-one courses all around India. The student was already being earmarked as a teacher.

'That is what really improved my coaching, because I had not done the base course. Level one was about the basic foundations. Understanding biomechanics is one thing, but understanding the basics is totally different . . . I would have taught close to

150 classes, and my expertise was bowling. So, the basics were firmly entrenched. When you have a lot of people asking you questions, that helps your thinking. My dissertation, by the way, was on spin bowling,' Arun said.

Coaching was now fast turning into Arun's passion. He was fascinated by the biomechanics and the player–management component not just in cricket but across all sports. He started reading books written by legendary American coaches such as John Wooden and Phil Jackson.

One quote from Wooden would be inked in Arun's mind forever and became the cornerstone of his coaching philosophy: 'A good coach expects a player to think highly of him, but a great coach helps a player think highly of himself.'

Arun's hard work and dedication was rewarded when he was offered a role at the National Cricket Academy (NCA) in Bangalore as a specialist bowling coach. He was also appointed the coach of the India A team along with the under-19 team. Under his tutelage, India won the 2012 World Cup in Australia.

'Those six years at the NCA [2007–14] was the golden period for me to gain knowledge and be exposed to different situations. I saw so many videos and bowlers with all sorts of actions. I also became the head coach of the team so was aware of what was required to coach a "team".'

★ ★ ★

During those foundational years, Arun would work with the likes of Umesh Yadav, Varun Aaron, Jasprit Bumrah, Bhuvneshwar Kumar and others, who would eventually go on to play starring roles in Indian cricket's fast bowling revolution.

His interactions with this lot would hold him in good stead. It meant that in his first formal appearance as a bowling coach in 2014, a lot of the faces were familiar. However, being an Indian bowling coach was another world altogether as compared to operating at the NCA.

'I knew most of the guys, expect for M.S. Dhoni and Mohammed Shami. The rest had all been part of the A tours or had been at the NCA frequently . . . They mainly came to the NCA to rework or fine-tune a few technical aspects, while with the Indian team it was more about practical output. So my method was to get a complete analysis on opponent batters—their strengths and weaknesses. Then I would look at how it suits our bowlers to exploit the weaknesses or shortcomings of those batters. It was also about empowering the bowler to think for himself how he would get a particular bowler out.'

One of the first lessons Arun had learnt in his coaching regimen was to form trust. So, slowly, he started to break down any barriers that existed and to form a strong bond with the likes of Shami, Bhuvneshwar Kumar and Varun Aaron. But just as he'd started to develop the connection, he would be asked to move on from his role, with Anil Kumble taking over as head coach in 2016.

'I was disappointed when I stopped. But I said, you can't stop me from coaching. And I got a chance with Hyderabad.'

It was a crucial run in Arun's career, and it also brought him closer to one of his early pet projects. It was he who had argued with the Hyderabad selectors to ensure that a fast bowler named Mohammad Siraj was picked in the Ranji Trophy team.

'I had seen Siraj at this camp. He was quick, and there were plenty of good attributes to his bowling. I asked, Why isn't this boy in the Ranji Trophy team squad? I got all sorts of answers, including stuff like, "He has a bad temperament." I told them, "Leave that to me. That is my job as the coach. But pick this boy, he is good."'

It was Siraj's first full season in the Ranji Trophy, and the youngster snared 41 wickets at 18.92 under the watchful eye of Arun. It would also be the first instance in the Ranji Trophy when three fast bowlers from one team had collectively taken 110 wickets for the season.

Hyderabad would go down narrowly to Mumbai in the quarterfinal that season, but Arun had enhanced his coaching credentials and, in the process, unearthed another fast bowler, primed and ready for the national call, in Siraj.

★ ★ ★

Back in 2014–15, on his first Test mission as the Indian bowling coach, for Arun it was more about finding the new mantra, one that the newly appointed Test captain was already keen to instil.

'Certainly, we have a lot to learn from the Australian bowlers. Especially someone like Josh Hazlewood [who had made his debut in that series]. He put the ball in the right spots in all three matches. That's something we need to learn, big time,' Virat Kohli had said with almost grudging admiration for Australia's ability to produce Test-ready fast bowlers.

India had done admirably well in the series with the bat, but despite having a settled bowling unit that included Ishant Sharma, Mohammed Shami, Umesh Yadav, Bhuvneshwar Kumar, Varun Aaron and Ravichandran Ashwin, the visiting bowlers had struggled to contain the Australian batters. Steve Smith, in particular, had plundered runs right through the series. No doubt, the pitches were benign, but for Kohli, who had seen Hazlewood rise so rapidly, it felt like there was something to be replicated by the Indian bowlers as a collective. Especially the way in which the tall New South Welshman was able to be consistent and relentless with his line and length.

It didn't help that India was captained by Kohli in the first Test and by Dhoni in the next two; and then Kohli would formally be anointed as the new leader from the fourth Test onwards in Sydney, following Dhoni's shock retirement from Test cricket.

'They were different as captains. Dhoni would say, "You prepare the bowlers, and I will manage them." Dhoni handled the bowlers on the field. He could read situations beautifully and handle bowlers accordingly. I told Dhoni about all the aspects that we'd discussed in the bowlers' team meeting, and then he would take it from there. And Kohli would want to be in the meeting, and know what we were discussing and how we were constructing the plans. So, they were completely different characters, but each had their own way of dealing with players,' said Arun.

The change of guard, with Kohl taking over, meant that Arun could construct a plan, having now realized that his vision matched that of the new captain. One of the first aspects was to understand each individual and what empowered each of them to succeed. 'What we had was Virat Kohli who was so passionate about Test cricket. He told Ravi from the outset, "Ravi Bhai, we have to be the best Test-playing nation in the world, and you just tell me what or how we can go about it. We will make it happen."'

Another one of Arun's coaching philosophies, and one he believes in strongly, was to 'coach the player and not the sport'. This meant building a rapport and establishing trust, which enabled the player to open up about not just his cricket but his life beyond cricket too.

Arun said: 'The coach concept in India almost paints them as a "man with the whip", but that had to change, and for that I had to be inclusive with all the bowlers. I had to trust them, and they had to trust me. But also, I needed to be a taskmaster, so we knew what we were trying to achieve; not just them but we as a collective. That eventually led to my becoming more like a friend, an elder brother or an adviser for them . . . It started with Virat and Ravi wanting this team to be the best. Then us identifying what characteristics were needed for the team to excel in all conditions, and sincerely working towards it.

'For us, it meant setting up challenges during practice. There is no point practising for hours on your comfort levels. If we can design a practice programme where the skills that are not your best get challenged, then we will improve. Each player would think about ways to improve, and we were always there to assist.

But for that, you had to throw them into the deep end all the time. Practice was the best place to do that, so a real match becomes an extension of your net.'

When a bowler came to the nets, Arun would ask the individual what he was trying to execute. He would then provide feedback to the player and give them a mark on a scale of 1–10. The players were told from the outset that they would be judged harshly and that they would need to be perfectionists to obtain a score of 10.

But just as the building blocks were being laid and a plan was in construction, Arun was out of the dressing room for eighteen months. When he returned in 2017, it was well and truly Virat Kohli's dressing room, which meant the head coach, the captain and Arun were all on the same page. Now, it was all about putting the plans they had discussed earlier into practice.

'The art of coaching is talking to the bowlers without discussing too many basics, because the player is not interested, unless there is a very studious bowler, like Ashwin. Others, like Shami, won't care. All they are concerned about is how the ball gets to the other end and what it does, and this is all that matters.

'With some bowlers, it was more a case of inception. You talk about different options and then tell them, "*Tere bowling se tu ye expose kar sakta hai kya* (Can you expose these particular weaknesses of a batter with your bowling)?" Then they would understand and seek advice as to how they could go about doing it. There needs to be a two-way communication chain, rather than simply me telling him to just go and do it. Make them think about it and why they can do it. Then they would feel they had conjured up the plan rather than you. And that would mean that they would take more ownership of the plan, irrespective of whether or not they executed it to a level of perfection . . . If they ever felt like they needed to do something instinctively, then I would give them the option to go ahead with it, as long as they could tell me the purpose of it. There should be no right or wrong.'

When a bowler got it wrong, Arun would ask what had gone through his mind while he chose a particular option. If the reply was based on some strategy the bowler thought of while on the field, the coach would encourage it. But if the bowler didn't exploit it consistently, then he would discuss it further.

'When it's Test cricket, you are against the best in the world, you may execute your plans well, but there will be times when the batters will still get away with it.'

According to Arun, the turning point in India's fast bowling revolution was the 2018 tour of South Africa. Over a period of time, he had learnt and realized what empowered and encouraged each bowler in the team and made them click. And from Shami to Bumrah to Ishant Sharma and Umesh Yadav, his approach had to be very different.

★ ★ ★

'Shami loves talking about bowling. He wants to give you the impression he knows it all. It is all about the way you build the relation with him. Ask him about his family or his upbringing. He is the guy who likes to talk about where he came from and the people he grew up with. When you speak in general there is a connection. To coach, you need to connect with the player at a level where you understand what their passion is and what drives them. When they know you genuinely care about them as a person and not just as a cricketer, it helps build that trust. Then you can challenge them,' Arun said.

And that's where Arun feels he really began to get the best out of Shami, whom he hadn't known as well as most of the other fast bowlers.

'Shami would casually say, "*Haan, sir, main toh woh plan kar sakta hoon* (Yes, sir, I can execute that plan)." Then I would tell him to execute it in the nets by bowling five balls on exactly the same spot. At the same time, I would also reinforce that if he didn't get one right, then I would come after him. While I was serious, it came across to him more like banter rather than me cracking the whip.

'You needed to cajole him and almost challenge him by saying, "*Tu ye nahi kar sakta hai* (You can't do this)." Then he would be like, "*Ye toh chhoti si baat hai, sir* (This is such a small matter, sir)." To which I would respond with, "*Chhoti si baat hai toh karke dikha* (If it is so trivial and easy, then do it and show me).'"

Arun had found a way to get the best out of Shami. And there were times when he didn't mind pushing the envelope.

'In the early stages of working with Shami, we had observed he kept bowling no-balls or started spells with half-volleys. We had data on what he did with each ball. I pulled him aside and went, "What's with these juicy volleys? Don't you have any dedication?" with a cuss word thrown in there, just to get him going.

'He has come a long way since that 2014 tour. But with Shami, you still have to remind him what he can do, otherwise he can deviate or get slightly too relaxed. One morning in Johannesburg, on that green-top in 2018, I said, "*Tere mein dam nahi hai* (You don't have it in you). Look at this pitch. You keep bowling at 132 kmph. What's the point? Show me what you have." The next day he took six wickets. We have made him work his backside off, to become what he is, and credit to him for turning his game around.'

Arun had to deal with Bumrah slightly differently. India's No. 1 fast bowler, Bumrah is a more 'serious' character, and Arun also found him to be a little 'touchy' and sensitive.

'To him, all I had to say was, "We need to try this. What do you think?" I would say that I was going to be really harsh in my feedback, and he would be like, "Fine, no problem." If I convinced Bumrah about a plan, he would ask a few questions, but once he was convinced, there was no looking back.'

But there were times when Arun had to give it straight to his main man, to get the best out of him. He takes us back to the fourth morning of the final Test in Sydney from 2019: 'Bumrah had bowled well, but when he came in the next morning, I told him, "This is such a benign pitch. Last night you were very good, at 137 kmph, but if you can make something happen with bowling at 137, imagine what you can do at your best. How people will talk about you if you can bring this pitch to life." He got the message. Next morning, the speed was touching 145 kmph again.'

It was more of a challenge when it came to convincing someone of Ishant Sharma's experience, considering that the lanky seamer had already become the senior bowler in the camp when Arun came in.

'With Ishant, it was difficult to convey the message at times. You had to almost lay your cards on the table. I said, "Look, your spells are economical, but out of 100 balls, how many are you making them play?" During the England tour in 2018, he was adamant that he was doing it right, so I said, "Just come with me for one session. I promise it will not spoil your bowling. I will show you what you can do in that one session. It has nothing to do with your action. It is simply about changing the angle you deliver from."

'I felt that his wrist was slightly in a pre-cocked action, which he could use to his advantage, especially for the inswinger. He ended up coming to the session. Ravi was also there, and we showed him the videos and the direction he was bowling from, and got him to deliver 10–15 balls from a different area on the crease, so that he could see where the ball was going. Then we said, "Look, with a slight change you will make the batters play a lot more. That is the best example of seeing is believing. Instead of going close to the stumps, deliver from the middle of the crease."'

The minor change had an immediate impact, as Ishant picked up five wickets in the second innings of the first Test at Edgbaston. And he would also credit Arun for his success at the post-match conference, saying, 'In the bowling meeting we spoke, and the bowling coach told me to straightaway come round the stumps, because the batsman finds it tough to play from that angle, because when my ball starts to swing, then it is difficult for left-handed batsmen.'

Another member of the pace attack who'd been in the Test squad for a while before Arun came along was Umesh Yadav.

Arun gave him the moniker 'Strongman' and found him to be very receptive to new ideas as well as fair criticism.

'You have to tell Umesh the tough points. When I saw him bowling in the nets and saw half-volleys on leg stump, I would say I saw ten of them in thirty-six balls. "That is potentially ten boundaries. We can't have that."'

Yadav missed out on getting a spot in the playing XI in the opening Test of the 2018–19 tour of Australia, despite having claimed eleven wickets in his previous Test in Hyderabad. Yadav justifiably wanted answers as to why he was left out.

'The answer was simple. Unless you can show me in practice that you can stop bowling half-volleys and not give away 20–40 runs in a spell, I can't pick you. He got it immediately, and we started seeing a different Umesh, not just in the nets, but also whenever he got a chance, like even this time in Adelaide,' said Arun.

There's a bit of Arun that wishes he could have worked a lot more with Bhuvaneshwar Kumar on the Test side of things. The two had, after all, known each other since the swing bowler played at the under-16 level. With Bhuvaneshwar, it was never an issue with bowling; it was more about pushing him in getting his body stronger and fitter.

'The strength and conditioning coach, Shankar Basu, and I would convey similar messages to Bhuvi but in a different manner. Then he started to believe the methods of training and worked really hard for six months on his body. The results were there for everyone to see, because after that, for about eighteen months, he was bowling close to 140 kmph in a consistent manner.'

The one bowler that Arun claims to have incidentally learnt from the most is, of course, Ashwin. He was the bowler who would challenge the bowling coach's abilities all the time and keep him honest and on his feet.

'Ashwin would ask a hundred questions. Ashwin is so intelligent that way, it forces you to think and have a solution. He would try so many different things. I actually learnt a lot by trying to convince someone at the international level to keep evolving like Ashwin always has. And to give him constructive feedback, I needed to constantly be on top of my game too.'

Arun also brought a slightly different approach to training sessions from what we'd seen before. He has always been a strong believer that what happens in the nets cannot be separated fully from what will happen in the middle. And Arun's one rule at every net session with India was that his bowlers were always bowling at full throttle.

'I would tell them, "If you are in the nets, you need to bowl at your top speed. If that is 145 kmph, I want to see you bowl at 145 kmph or don't bowl at all." And bowling no-balls was a big no-no during practice sessions.'

He recalls having worked with both Bumrah and Shami on getting them to bowl fewer no-balls than before. 'Why does anyone bowl a no-ball: they overstride because of adrenaline and rhythm, or wind or a downhill slope. I would tell them, "You just go out and bowl. I'm there to observe. Don't worry if you bowl a no-ball at the start of the session in the nets. Go flat out and just tell me when you have found top rhythm." I would watch it for a couple of balls and at times observe the spot he was starting his run-up from, and after several observations, ask him to adjust that spot by a metre at the max, either forward or back. That would become his new starting point and eliminate the chances of his overstepping considerably.'

The England tour of 2018 was the biggest learning curve for Arun as the bowling coach. India lost the series 4–1, but the way the pace bowlers performed was a sign that they were close to being the finished product. Over a period of time, all the discussions he'd had with his bowlers had helped build trust. The bowlers started saying, '*Paaji [Arun] bolega toh theek hi rahega, so hum wo first try karenge* (If Arun says something, it must be right, and we are willing to try it).' That he had the entire bowling group now working towards the same goal also meant he could start empowering them a lot more.

The improvement in terms of consistency on the tours of South Africa and England in 2018 provided the coaching staff with enough belief to conquer Australia in 2018–19. Four years on, from Kohli having looked over at the Australian camp with a bit of envy in terms of their fast-bowling prowess, it was the Aussies who looked on in awe at the growing might of India as a fast-bowling nation.

By the time India returned for the 2020–21 series, Arun had been in the Indian system for over two decades. He had worked with so many bowlers that he knew exactly what was required to empower a bowler to ensure they executed a specific plan.

So when Shastri called Arun that evening in August, asking him to devise a plan for Australia based on his 'leg-side' theory, he could construct the master plan knowing India had the bowlers at their disposal to execute it.

Arun said, 'Bumrah can be used to bowl those lines. Shami could have been used like that had Ishant been there; he would have been ideal for it. Siraj was cut out to bowl those lines because his primary ball is the one that comes back in after pitching. Even Saini, who bowls slightly wider from the crease, was suited to bowling that line.' And the fact that they could stick with it, despite the spate of injuries to their key bowlers, was a sign of Arun's influence over the bowling group as a whole—not just on the incumbents but also on those rising through the ranks.

★ ★ ★

The friendship between Ravi Shastri and Bharat Arun went back to their junior cricket days. They'd first met as part of the India under-19 team in 1981, on a tour to Sri Lanka, where Shastri was captain. They'd also then spent a summer playing league cricket for Morecambe, where Arun was a semi-professional and Shastri the professional player. Living in the same house for months on end, and experiencing life together at that crucial age, only brought them closer. While they'd always stayed in touch, it was only after they came together in the Indian dressing room that they really started spending a lot of time together after nearly three decades. And while Arun was officially the bowling coach from the very beginning, his role went well beyond just getting the bowlers ready for battle.

From the day he was introduced to the rest of the team in glowing terms by Shastri in 2014, Arun had known that the two would have to work as a team, to not just win the trust of the dressing room but also connect at a deeper level with every member of the team. That required the two of them to work separately and together with each player. They were very different in their approaches yet managed to complement each other, and that is what Arun feels led to their eventual success as a coaching group. Their lifelong friendship and keenness to spend time with each other went a long way in that too.

'Our method was simple,' Arun said. 'We would observe them. Once they know you are not imposing on them, you meet them and socialize, talk about various topics. Once we have the trust, we can use the good cop–bad cop technique, even though I wouldn't call it that.

'Our aim was to be firm without being harsh. If a certain aspect needed firm words, we would have to do it. That was where our different personalities helped a lot. Ravi is more direct. While I would look at relaying a message by triggering a player, by getting them to think more about what was done or what needed to be done. The information coming from us, though, had to be the same. There could be no discrepancy in that.

'We also did our homework by discussing our respective approaches. If a certain player comes to me, then I figure a way out to relay the message; or if they go to Ravi, he can give them different options. If he was a batter, Ravi would talk to them more. If he was a bowler, then it would be me.'

And that brings us to another of Arun's tent-pole coaching philosophies: using the 'sandwich theory' to get his point across without putting too much pressure on a player.

'You basically start with talking about their fabulous performance, then slip in the point about where you think they need to improve or work on, and then top it up with more encouraging words, like how you know they'll be the best they can be.'

Arun also developed a strong bond with a number of senior batters in the team, and it reached a point where they started feeling comfortable getting into some friendly banter with him.

'I was close to most of them—to Rohit, Shikhar, KL and Puji,' said Arun. 'And while speaking to them, I could pick up on certain things, and I would pass that message on to Ravi. Then Ravi would deal with it directly or tell them to work with the batting coach in case it was something more technical in nature. Soon enough, the players also settled into that culture, knowing that there was no mistrust between the coaches.

'Our understanding was brilliant, so there was no insecurity. The trust was instantaneous, considering our friendship over so many years. We were also fortunate to have other coaches who trusted our approach. It always helped that Ravi never had any agenda. That meant that unlike in some other dressing rooms around the world, there was no insecurity among the assistant coaches; they didn't have to constantly look over their shoulder. As a coaching group, we were also very open about accepting our mistakes if we got anything wrong, which helped too.'

Arun's easy-going demeanour made him a lot more approachable for a number of younger players. Rishabh Pant, for one, never shied away from being his boisterous, funny self around the bowling coach. And the difference in how Shastri and Arun dealt with a player would come through especially when one of the players was having a tough time.

'Ravi, you know, is straight-to-the-point and is naturally a very inspirational person. I was more diplomatic, in some ways, where I would project it on the players and get them to open up and self-motivate. For that, I really believed strongly in getting them to feel free to discuss any issue they wanted to, whether it was from their childhood or the present. Learning about their early struggles was important, whether it was "Oh, my dad drank a lot, and my mother had to look after everything" or some other trauma. It said a lot about how a player would react to different scenarios on and off the field. But they also knew that we would always maintain that confidentiality, and this information would never leave that room.'

As Shastri would say in interviews later, Arun also became the guy who the head coach leaned on the most to keep his own sanity even in the most trying of circumstances. 'I couldn't have done this job for more than two years without Arun by my side. He was the one who kept me going and pulled me up at times when I was on the brink,' Shastri would say.

For all the good times, and not so good ones, that he experienced as one of the head coaches of the Indian team, it was his bonding with these young men at such a deep level that remains the most satisfying aspect of his coaching career to date.

He said, 'An ICC title during our time would have been the icing on the cake, yes, but to achieve what we did, especially winning in Australia in 2020–21 with the team we had, is something I couldn't have even dreamt of when I decided to try my hand at coaching all those years ago.' And Indian cricket is glad he did.

13

The Rise of Rishabh

'Sirji, am I playing?'

'NO!'

Next day, the same question and the same response.

It had become a sort of daily routine for Rishabh Pant and Ravi Shastri in the days leading up to the Adelaide Test. Wherever the head coach went, Pant was right there behind him, much to Bharat Arun's amusement. And so persistent was the ebullient wicketkeeper that eventually, even Shastri had started to see the funny side of it. Even if he remained very firm in his assessment of whether Pant was ready to take the gloves for the first Test.

'He was so keen to play. He would keep nagging Ravi. He would stand behind Ravi at training, and the minute Ravi turned around, Rishabh would have that mischievous smile and say, '*Aapko pata hai main peechhe kyun khada hoon* (You know why I am standing behind you)." And then say, "Am I playing?" How many people can go to the head coach and, jokingly or seriously, ask him these things? But that's just Rishabh,' Arun reminisced, still quite taken with Pant's impishness.

The second Shastri would say no, Pant was ready with his standard query: 'Sir, why not? I'm working so hard?' The head coach's reply was always the same too: 'You keep working hard, and there will be a chance for you to play.'

Pant had been a part of the team's plans as they prepared for Australia, but the minute they landed in Sydney the coaching staff had noticed that the naturally stocky wicketkeeper–batter was carrying a little bit of extra weight.

'When he came to the tour of Australia he was 6–7 kg overweight, maybe because there had been seven months of inactiveness due to Covid lockdowns. Ravi made sure Pant knew about it and told him, "Unless you trim down, and if you don't match the fitness standards, it will be difficult for you to play."'

Arun had noticed that Shastri's stern message early on the tour may have jolted Pant a little. Perhaps it wasn't what he was expecting to hear. So, Arun took the onus on himself to have a chat with him about it.

'I explained to him why he might have put on weight. It was the lockdown, and it was natural, since it was hard to go anywhere. I also told him, "You love to eat, and at times you don't know what to eat. So it is understandable." We were aware that he liked fast food. But I also reminded him that he had so much talent that all he needed to do was sacrifice somewhere a little, and basically start eating more sensibly.'

Arun wasn't done, though. It wasn't only about Pant's diet. He also wanted him to work harder than ever before on his fitness. And since Pant wasn't part of the white-ball squads, it also gave him more time to do so.

Arun's message to Pant was: 'This month I don't need you to work on your skills, because I know skill-wise you have it. Instead, work a lot more on wicketkeeping and training. The fitter person utilizes more of his talent because he stays fresh. There could be a stage at the backend of the game, where you have to run a hard three or you need to run two when batting with the tailenders, and if you're unfit, you can't do that.'

The Delhi dynamo took every bit of the bowling coach's advice on board and to heart. When he wasn't spending time in the gym, he was spotted running laps, literally all day long.

Having been ruled out of the practice match at the Drummoyne Oval with a stiff neck, Pant spent those three days running many laps of the Oval during each interval and practised his keeping when he wasn't doing that.

On the second day of that match, he even pestered Prithvi Shaw to throw him a few balls on the sidelines. When Shaw had had enough, Pant convinced him to throw a few more with an effective and cute little barter. '*Aur de na thoda. Chal aur dega toh uske baad tujhe wicketkeeping gloves doonga, aur main throw karoonga* (Give me some more. I promise, if you give me more, I will let you wear my keeping gloves, and I will throw to you).'

Shaw took up the offer and, in return, would also get a few pointers. The pair would share a laugh at the end of it. The disappointment of missing out on the first practice game didn't bring down Pant's energy or boisterousness by any level. When he wasn't creating a lot of noise in the dressing room, he was indulging in some self-deprecatory humour with Melinda Farrell and me about his running routines. He also drew the ire of one of the security guards when he grabbed a phone from one of the Indian fans from outside the stadium who had asked for a selfie— technically, it was a minor bubble breach. But he got away with it, like only Rishabh Pant can.

While Pant continued to sharpen his skills with the gloves, he made the most of his chance to remind the coaching staff of what they had on their cards by scoring a dazzling ton at the SCG in the second tour match.

He had the entire dressing room, including Kohli, on his feet, and maybe it only prompted him to nag Shastri a bit more. He eventually took being left out of the Adelaide pans on the chin and continued to work really hard behind the scenes.

On the eve of the Test match, the practice session was optional, but Pant was among the first people there. And it wasn't in the nets where he would sweat it out; instead, he continued to work on his wicketkeeping drills and a few sprints. As the team disappeared into

the sheds, the only two people left on the ground were Pant and
Jadeja. The spin-bowling all-rounder, too, was slowly regaining his
fitness after a hamstring injury.

Pant had ensured that the team management simply couldn't
ignore him for the next Test match. Of course, in between the
sprints and the drills, he carried on doing several backflips and
handstands. He never stopped being Rishabh Pant.

★ ★ ★

The first sign that Pant would be displacing Wridhiman Saha came
during the practice sessions in Melbourne. The keeper spent close
to an hour in the middle of the MCG working on high catches and
then having long stints in the nets. As he faced up to the bowlers,
it was evident to us watching from 4–5 meters away that he was
really switched-on. Generally, there would be that slight casualness
while he batted in the nets, but here he looked determined and
asked a lot of questions to the bowlers as to what their fields were
and, after being beaten by a ball from Ashwin, if Pant 'could have
left that'.

Pant would also extend his batting sessions, sneaking in
whenever there was an opening and screaming, 'I'm backkkk' at
the reserve bowlers. He would also pester Raghu constantly to test
him with a barrage of bouncers. He was also always in Ashwin's
ear while facing the off spinner, asking him for feedback about his
batting against spin.

After India's horrible batting display in Adelaide and with
Pant looking in the right shape, both mentally and physically, the
coaching staff had no option but to include him in the playing XI
for the second Test. Plus, his being a left-hander and his previous
record in Australia were always going to help his case. But one
question remained, over whether he would bat at No. 6 or No. 7.

'The number-six slot was ideal for him. The perfect situation
for us was that Rishabh would come in around that 45–50 over

mark. The ball had gone old, and, especially in Australia, it is the best time to bat and score runs quickly. If Rishabh batted during that time, we could add 100–140 runs in quick time. He could really bat with freedom. Plus, we had Jadeja at number seven, who could handle the second new ball,' said Arun.

Things would pan out exactly the way the team had envisaged. Pant walked out to the crease in the forty-fourth over at the MCG. He would only make 29 off 40 balls, but his presence at the crease bolstered the Indian run rate and gave the innings a bit of momentum, which Ajinkya Rahane and Ravindra Jadeja took advantage of to put India ahead in the match.

'Even in Test cricket he is going to go after the bowling. The best thing for Rishabh is, his shots fetch high value in Tests because of the attacking fields. He thrives when the fields are attacking. Many opposition teams don't have an answer to a batsman like that in the longer format. Do I attack or defend? And by the time they get it right, he has got to sixty or seventy runs. He has done it more often than any other cricketer in recent times; his record is phenomenal. He is very similar to Adam Gilchrist,' Arun said.

Pant had won Australia over on his first visit here during the 2018–19 summer—whether it was with his wit behind the stumps or with the unbridled excitement he brought to the crease with bat in hand. And the Gilchrist comparisons had started right away.

The two had never crossed paths before. And as it turned out, it was Gilchrist who, funnily enough, initiated their first meeting, during the previous Indian tour of Australia in 2018–19. Pant's reaction, when he finally came face to face with his idol, would leave the Indian support staff member who'd introduced them completely stunned: 'It was Pant's first tour of Australia. I was talking to Gilchrist in the lobby of the hotel. Gilchrist said to me something along the lines of, "Plenty of raps about that kid," pointing towards Pant. I couldn't believe that they hadn't met. So, I yelled out to Rishabh and told him to come over. But he just stood there. I walked over and said, "Come. Gilly wants to meet you." Pant's reaction was, "No, no. How can I talk to him? He is such a legend of the game. He has done so much. Who am I?" Finally, I dragged him over, and it was funny because it was almost like his Indian customs had taken over, and he was ready to touch Gilly's feet. For me, it said a great deal about how much Pant respected the game and those who'd played it before him. Gilly was completely taken with him too.'

Perhaps this was the interaction that Pant needed to inspire himself further to be the best in the world. To be the next Adam Gilchrist. And Suresh Raina was the first who'd hear about it.

* * *

Pant had spent an entire week with Raina in Ghaziabad and Delhi around July 2020. While they trained together, the youngster also used this time to talk about his ambitions and goals on and off the field. Raina was someone he'd always been close with.

Pant had come off a trying period with the bat, and many critics had written him off as a long-term international prospect. Raina had realized that, more than anything, Pant needed someone to put an arm around him and listen to him.

One day, Pant pulled Raina aside and said he'd made a declaration to himself. That he wanted to become the 'best wicketkeeper–batter in the world'. He'd said it in passing before, but Raina had never sensed the same level of conviction before. He wasn't just saying it this time. And in a few months, Pant would show how much he'd meant it.

'He did a lot of fitness work with me. With his batting, it wasn't technical at all. It was more about getting into the right mindset, and feeling good about his cricket and his enjoying his game,' Raina had told me in an interview in 2020.

A senior member of the team on the 2018–19 tour, who knows a thing or two about wicketkeeping, was really impressed by Pant. He wanted to ensure that Pant did justice to his talent and didn't slip up. Pant would be told, politely yet firmly, by this senior teammate that he was destined to be India's keeper for the next decade, and the only way he would lose his way would be if he ever became casual towards his approach in regard to fitness.

If Pant looked up to Gilchrist as an idol, he was also fortunate enough to have a mentor, a guru even, in Mahendra Singh Dhoni. There was an ODI against Australia in Ranchi in 2019, and while the rest of the team stayed in the five-star hotel, Pant spent those two days at the Dhoni residence.

There was a bond and a unique comfort level that they shared, despite Dhoni being fifteen years senior to him—a connection that seemed to have been forged on India's tour of West Indies in 2017.

It was the first tour for Pant with the senior team and a fun one too. Though he didn't get to play in any of the ODIs, he never left Dhoni's side during training. And halfway through that tour, he won over literally the entire dressing room simply by being himself. I remember being at the Sabina Park the evening before the solitary T20I on that tour, where the Indian batters were involved in a six-hitting battle to see who could hit the ball the farthest. This was where Pant's eagerness to not just fit in but to feel on a par with the rest of his senior teammates really came through. But he seemed to put so much pressure on himself to match some of the big-hitters that he kept mistiming balls, with hardly one or two even managing to go over the ropes and even the likes of batting coach Sanjay Bangar outdoing him. A nearly crestfallen Pant had started making his way back towards the dressing room soon after the session when Dhoni ran across, put an arm around him and cracked a joke, which lit up the teenager all over again as he went back to being Rishabh Pant.

★ ★ ★

Playing audacious shots has always been a part of Pant's approach to batting—whether it's the reverse ramp off James Anderson or the many other outrageous shots he pulled off against the English at Edgbaston in July 2022.

On India's tour of England in 2018, Pant was not in the playing XI and was there as the backup keeper to Dinesh Karthik. During the second Test at Lord's, Pant was having a net session at the back of the stand. A loud roar would grab his and a few other non-playing members' attention there. The information was relayed that Karthik had been bowled for a duck. It didn't bother Pant as he tried to smash the next ball out of the ground and reverse-swept the next two balls in the nets.

It prompted a senior member of the side, who was also on the outer at that stage, to walk over and say, 'Look, DK just got a low score. So now at least play properly. You could be playing in the next Test match. You never know.'

Pant's reply was pretty straightforward: 'Sirji, I play the same in the match as I do in the nets.'

Pant would debut in the next Test, and he would end up smashing the second ball he faced in Test cricket by running down the pitch and lofting Adil Rashid for a six over long on. Yes, he'd lived up to his word all right.

As a former national selector would later reveal, they weren't even planning on including Pant in the Test squad for the England series, but it was the way he had adapted his game against the Dukes ball during the A matches that prompted the selectors to reconsider. With scores of 3, 67 not out, 58 and 61 against the England Lions on tricky pitches, Pant had even taken India A coach Rahul Dravid by surprise.

'Pant is always going to be an attacking player, but reading of the situation when one is playing red-ball cricket is required, and Rishabh has shown here that he can bat differently,' Dravid had said at the time.

Those innings, and the development in his wicketkeeping, demonstrated to the selectors and the senior Indian team management that Pant was capable of adapting to any situation.

As a member of the Indian support staff says now, 'He is not as casual as people think. There is another side of Rishabh, the responsible side. I feel since he lost his father when he was seventeen or eighteen, he understood his responsibility not just in cricket but also outside it.'

He has had the reputation of being a maverick, on and off the field, a natural entertainer. It's always interesting to hear him respond to questions about being an entertainer with bat in hand: 'I don't know about that. I just play my way, and my focus is always on winning matches for my country. If people get entertained by it, then that's great.' And Arun understands where that comes from.

'He basically doesn't want anyone to think that he's just out there having fun. He plays his cricket very seriously, and winning matters a lot to him. It's just that the way he goes about winning is so entertaining that he gets asked about it all the time,' said Arun.

Seen from the outside, Rishabh Pant is your quintessential 'lives to entertain' kind of cricketer. The highlights in his hair, all the social media activity, and he's never shied away from his interest in expensive products. Before his Test debut, he was seen showing off to his teammates his branded leather shoes that he had purchased for an extraordinary amount. I remember interviewing him soon after he was picked up for a sizeable amount in the IPL while he was still a part of the India under-19 World Cup squad. When asked about what he would want to do with the money, he spoke about buying expensive cars and big houses. The candour was both refreshing and impressive. Here was a young man who knew what he wanted in life and how he could get it.

But along with that flair, there is also a softer, human side to him. Ironically, the day he was boasting about his expensive shoes, he was also seen giving food to homeless people waiting outside a restaurant.

What shines through, above all, is his loyalty and dedication towards the Indian cricket team and how he is prepared to sacrifice anything, including his own body, if it means winning matches for his country. And that takes us to the SCG nets on Day Four of the third Test.

* * *

It's a net session that I have written and spoken about quite a bit since it happened. But every time I do, it's just a reminder of the extent an athlete can go to in their quest for glory on the sporting field, especially in team sport, when it's more about what your achievement would mean for your team and your teammates.

There had been doubts over whether Pant could bat in the second innings after having received a very painful blow to the arm on Day Three. But with Jadeja having suffered a broken thumb, it was imperative for Pant, or so he felt, that he at least give himself a chance to have a hit.

Rohit Sharma and Shubman Gill had started off quite comfortably against the new ball and looked to be settling in nicely when I spotted, from the corner of my eye, that Pant was heading towards the SCG nets. Surprised as well as eager to see what condition his arm was in, I quietly slipped out of the press box and headed towards the practice area. Pant was there with two throwdown specialists while physio Nitin Patel kept a watchful eye on him.

It started off with the wicketkeeper trying to get bat to ball and see how badly it impacted the pain he was already suffering from. And it became obvious that it was exacerbating the pain greatly. Having started off batting with the strap over his arm, he chucked it away and tried to face up to the pain even more.

While some shots seemed to hurt more, there were others where he simply grimaced and grit his teeth. Through it all, he kept smiling and laughing, and encouraging Nuwan to chuck faster and more at his body. He would even start taunting the throwdown specialists, saying, 'Don't get scared, increase the pace.' He would then turn around to the physio, who was by now standing beside the net, and tell him that the support staff was scared of hurting him.

His elbow took the brunt of the bat's impact with the ball, but he kept shaking off the pain. Whenever Patel looked away, I heard Pant muttering to himself under his breath, '*Chal, chal tujhe kuch nahi hua hai* (Come on, you're fine, nothing has happened to you),' in a bid to fight off, or rather ignore, the pain.

The Test match was still going on in the middle, with Rohit and Gill continuing to hold the Aussies at bay. There was a makeshift marquee behind the nets at the SCG during that summer for the corporate guests with a couple of TV sets installed inside. So, apart from being an intrepid nets watcher, I also had to double up as mime artist every time Pant or the others heard the crowd react inside the SCG and wanted an update on what had happened. I would watch the screen and then let them know, using nothing more than gestures, if it was a boundary or someone being beaten outside the off stump or an LBW appeal. I also had to use facial expressions to let them know who the batter on strike was.

Then they were back to it. It was only when Pant began to get semi-annoyed with his throwdown specialists for not testing him with short balls at full speed that they began to do exactly what he wanted of them. '*Wahaan bouncer hi daalenge* (They're going to bowl only bouncers at me in the middle),' he told Nuwan, the Hindi-speaking Sri Lankan, at one point. Some twenty-five minutes into the session, the head physio seemed satisfied that Pant would be able to battle through the pain the next day. And they left the net with Patel saying, 'It'll be a surprise that will hit them hard. It'll be a big surprise.' We know now what that surprise was and also how it ended.

But we also know now how this incredible show of 'guts and gumption', as he soldiered on through the pain for his country's sake, was Rishabh Pant laying the marker for what was to come, not just on this tour but, probably, for the next decade or so.

He would no longer have to nag an Indian coach or follow him around to get his place back in a Test playing XI.

14

Gabbatoir Has Fallen

'*Ravi Bhai, Nattu toh badiya daal raha hai? Khila do usse* (Ravi Bhai, Natarajan is bowling really well. Just play him).'

It was two days before the start of the series. Ravi Shastri had stopped by for a chat en route to the visitors' dressing room at the Adelaide Oval. India had finished a late training session, where T. Natarajan had been the pick of the bowlers. He'd troubled every Indian batter, including captain Virat Kohli.

Shastri looked at me, as if he was taking my borderline-ridiculous suggestion into consideration. A wink and a nod later, he turned to his bowling coach Bharat Arun and went, '*Arey Baaat, Nattu ko bhi khila dein ek Test match* (Should we give Natarajan a Test match too)?' We all laughed a hearty laugh that evening in Adelaide.

I wouldn't venture to say that the joke was on us eventually. In a way it was, though. For, as we got to the Gabba, it wasn't so much a case of whether they wanted to hand T. Natarajan a Test cap; it was more that they had no choice but to hand him his Test cap.

To really fathom the absurdity of the idea that Natarajan would be taking the new ball in the fourth Test on 15 January, you had to look at where he stood in the pecking order on 15 December.

Yes, he had gone on to make his ODI and T20I debut after having started the tour as a reserve. But back in Adelaide, India were starting out with Jasprit Bumrah, Mohammed Shami and Umesh Yadav. They had Mohammad Siraj primed and ready to step in if needed. So, too, Navdeep Saini, who'd come close to playing in Christchurch earlier that year. Right outside the original squad sat Shardul Thakur, desperate to reignite his Test career after the false start in 2018. And even the young Kartik Tyagi for that matter, considering how impressive he'd been against Australia A at Drummoyne Oval.

It was not like Natarajan himself was thinking about all this. He was having the time of his life already, running in and bowling at the superstars of Indian cricket, beating them and getting plaudits from them. We would even hear him let out a 'yesss' under his breath every time he got an outside edge off Rohit Sharma or Cheteshwar Pujara.

There was no official confirmation about Natarajan playing in Brisbane. In fact, on the morning of the match, Brad Haddin and I sat in the SEN studios in Sydney, peering into the TV screen, trying to spot any hints of India's playing XI.

At times it meant ignoring what the legendary Robert 'Crash' Craddock was saying live on camera from the Gabba and looking past him. While I made the rookie error of looking at the players' faces to gauge their moods, Haddin, with all his experience, was looking at their shoes. He suddenly spotted one pair and nudged me saying, 'That guy is in. He's got bowling shoes on,' only to realize that the 'guy' was Natarajan, whom Haddin had worked with as part of Sunrisers Hyderabad.

So that was one mystery solved. Incredibly, Natarajan's selection wasn't even the biggest surprise of the day. He had at least been added to the Test squad before the Sydney game. And he had been playing first-class cricket for Tamil Nadu over the past few seasons.

Washington Sundar hadn't played a long-form game at that level for over three years. India had officially reached in and found the 'last man standing'.

The twenty-one-year-old all-rounder had, after all, been held back with the Test squad purely so that he could replicate Nathan Lyon during practice. He was not even a full-fledged net bowler, considering that at most times all he did was roll his arm over from a solitary position to create the Lyon effect.

Somewhere in Chennai, there was someone who believed that Washington would end up playing a Test match before returning home from Australia. And when M.S. Sundar revealed his clairvoyance to the rest of the family, neither Washington's mother nor his sister knew what to make of it. The young Tamil Nadu cricketer didn't know what to tell his father either when the latter told him about this premonition over a phone call. All Washington was looking for was a Happy New Year greeting.

I remember speaking to Washington's sister, Shailaja, a cricketer herself, on the day the stylish left-hander would dig India out of trouble in his very first Test innings. And amid a lot of sibling banter, she described the scenes around the Sundar household that morning with extreme glee.

They had learnt about his shock debut a day earlier over a video call, and the alarms had been set for 3.15 a.m. for the morning of the Test. They didn't want to miss a single moment of that momentous day, starting with R. Ashwin handing Washington his Test cap in the Indian huddle. Interestingly, there was another apt candidate to lead the cap-presentation ceremony at the Gabba that morning. Except that Sridharan Sriram, who had handed a very young Washington his club cap in Chennai a few years prior, was in the opposition camp here.

And then there was Shardul Thakur, the guy who had turned down the Diwali sweets cooked at the Joshi household on the third day of quarantine to ensure that he maintained his fitness right through to the end of the tour—just in case his services were required. (As someone who has indulged a lot in the sweets made at the Joshi household, trust me when I say that it's not easy to say no to them.) So here was that chance for Thakur, a second coming in Test cricket.

It meant that India's bowlers at the Gabba, where Australia had not lost for thirty-five years, had a combined experience of four Tests between the five of them. Mohammad Siraj had never bowled with a cricket ball before 2015, and Navdeep Saini only did so for the first time in 2012. In what should be hailed as the ultimate triumph for all those tennis-ball cricket tournaments around the country, here they were leading the attack for India as the senior-most members of the bowling line-up.

* * *

'HEADDDD UP!' Ravi Shastri's booming voice resonated right across and around the mostly empty restaurant in Hamilton. It was February 2020, and we were in New Zealand for India's month-long tour right before the pandemic. He was seated by the bar with his partner-in-crime, bowling coach Bharat Arun.

The order, which sounded more like a military command, was directed at Shardul Thakur. The all-rounder from Mumbai was just about to step out of the restaurant after having finished dinner with a bunch of his teammates at the other end of the room. While the rest of the group seemed in good spirits, Shastri had noticed that Thakur wasn't quite himself. His broad shoulders seemed to be a tad slouched and the customary wide smile was missing too. So he summoned Thakur over for a brief pep talk.

It was the night after the first ODI at Seddon Park. In a high-scoring contest, the Kiwis had chased down 348 with just under two overs to spare. Thakur had been, by far, the most expensive of the bowlers, conceding 80 runs in his nine overs. Shastri wanted to make sure that his energetic fast bowler wasn't letting the minor setback impact him too much.

The words of advice were as sharp as they were succinct. With his arm around him, Shastri asked Thakur to be the first one out at practice the following morning. 'I want you there with your chest puffing out and running in full steam like it matters. Do that, and you'll see how things start looking up for you. Just make sure that your head always stays up. One off day can't lead to your head dropping. *Abhi jaa, champion* (Off you go now),' Shastri was overheard telling Thakur.

It was almost a different Shardul Thakur that you saw for the rest of that tour. Not only was there an extra spring in his stride, but he was also beginning to feel a lot more integral to the vibe of the Indian dressing room. This was, of course, well before his transformation into a cult hero. He had played all of four ODIs for the country in the two years leading up to that tour. There also seemed to be an increased level of self-confidence, despite the rest of the series going neither his nor India's way.

In fact, I even remember his being rather brusque with me when I had mentioned his disappointing Test debut from 2018— where he suffered a groin strain after bowling only ten deliveries— during a press conference in Mt Maunganui. My question was loosely about if he thought he would ever get such a chance again in the longer format.

'I have forgotten about that already. I'm not sure why you want to bring it up now. I don't live in the past,' he had shot back something to that effect. Though a little taken aback, I took it as a sign that Shastri's inspirational discourse that night in Hamilton had worked. Thakur's head was never going to drop again.

And it didn't drop even for a moment while he waited for his turn to play in the Border–Gavaskar Trophy, some ten months on from the rousing pep talk in that bar on Victoria Street. Thakur had been held back with the touring party for the Tests as one of the net bowlers. At times, he even came across like a human bowling machine. Every Indian practice session you went to, there he was among the first few players to walk into the nets and start warming up. By the time the usual first lot of tailenders was done with their batting stints, Thakur was ready at the top of his mark with a new ball in hand.

'Shardulllll,' the war cry would ring from Shastri, reverberating around the practice area and maybe even in the streets outside the venue, as soon as K.L. Rahul or Mayank Agarwal were done marking their guard. And off went Thakur, beginning a two-hour-long spell of relentless intensity and hostility. He'd stay as competitive and combative with his final delivery as he had been with his first. There were no let-ups. It didn't matter who the batter was. Shardul Thakur would take on all—and get fired up especially if it was one of the senior members of the side.

One hot afternoon at the MCG, he spent nearly twenty minutes steaming in and bowling bouncer after bouncer at Rohit Sharma, challenging the opener to take him on. And every time Rohit missed, Thakur was there right under his nose, letting his fellow Mumbaikar know that he was in a contest. Rohit wasn't prepared to take a step back either, and the battle continued for a good while. By this stage, Thakur had already bowled for well over eighty minutes and was so involved in this showdown that he even forgot to stop for a drink.

Following Shami's departure, Thakur had been officially added to the Test squad. There were even some signs in the days leading up to the third Test—especially during the full-fledged training sessions that India continued to have in Melbourne before heading to Sydney—that Thakur might get the nod ahead of Navdeep Saini. But it wasn't to be. It's safe to say that the seamer wasn't too chuffed about it. Not that he made it known through his body language. Test recall or not, in the nets he kept steaming in, spell after spell, like his life depended on it. But those close to him would reveal that he did feel a tad slighted by the team's decision.

Navdeep Saini had bowled arguably the quickest spell of the tour by anyone, across both teams, in the nets during one of the training sessions in Melbourne. It was so rapid that you didn't feel safe creeping up too close to the net, purely because of the intensity with which the ball kept thudding into it. It seemed only a matter of time before one would burst through and smash you in the face. Below us, the Indian batters who had to contend with Saini that day were looking equally uneasy—ducking and weaving out of the thunderbolts that the Haryana pacer was unleashing at them. Pujara, in particular, spent most of the session with his back turned towards the clear Melbourne skies, leaving and ducking deliveries. It's safe to say that Saini had earned his way into the playing XI with this burst on that day, and the team management was considering him as the third seamer for the third Test. Thakur's name, too, came up for discussion, and he was even seen having a long hit in his Chennai Super Kings yellow-and-gold gloves. But he would have to wait another week.

Through it all, Thakur remained undeterred. And when news came that Bumrah had indeed been ruled out of the Gabba Test, owing to the abdominal strain, the time had come for Thakur to reap the just rewards for having been the unsung warrior behind the scenes. It was fitting that Thakur would return to test cricket in Queensland, as it was to this northern state of Australia that he had travelled in 2016 from across the globe, in the space of thirty-six hours, to play for India A.

Gaurav was part of the commentary team for that India A tour and recalls how Thakur had told him about his journey from Port of Spain in Trinidad to Kingston in Jamaica, on to London and then Delhi, where he had to collect his Australian visa documents in person before flying immediately to Mumbai. He would hardly have time to pack his bags before boarding a flight from Mumbai to Singapore, then onwards to Mackay via Brisbane. It was a severely jet-lagged Thakur who finally arrived in Mackay, having travelled close to 30,000 km in around forty hours.

So, when the then India A coach, Rahul Dravid, asked Thakur if he was ready to play the next morning, the reply was prompt: 'I didn't travel across the world to miss a match for India A. One day, I want to be playing for my country, so there is no way I'm missing the game tomorrow. I will be fine.'

This was just one example of Thakur's pragmatism and his forthrightness.

Gaurav also remembers the time he met Thakur during the IPL. Thakur told him that he was heading to his hometown of Palghar for a day. When asked why he was planning on boarding a crowded train instead of driving there, the burly all-rounder almost seemed bemused. 'What's the point of driving? The traffic is so bad it takes me 3–4 hours. The train is far more convenient. I board at Bombay Central and reach Palghar in one and a half hours. You just have to be practical.'

'Be Practical' could well be the title of a book on his life and career someday.

Thakur has always believed in playing matches rather than training in the nets or in the gym. There was an instance when a national selector had assured him of a place in the playing XI for an Irani Trophy match, only to be told on the morning of the match that he would not feature in it. Thakur was irritated by the miscommunication purely due to the fact that he was keen on some game time, having just recovered from an injury. Such was his dedication to the task that he fielded for a couple of days before attaining permission to play in a club match the following day and then returning to field again on the final day.

All those deliveries in the nets, the toil in domestic cricket and, not to forget, the crazy travel must have seemed worth it when Thakur got the nod to resume his Test career in Brisbane. He was the first bowler to grab the bucket of paint to mark out of his run-up at both the Stanley Street and the Vulture Street ends.

★ ★ ★

For all the grand plans India had laid out for the Australian tour, Thakur was perhaps the one bowler in the camp not best suited to execute the leg-side theory, being a swing bowler. But in true Shardul Thakur fashion, the first ball he delivered on his comeback was clipped by Marcus Harris in the air straight to square leg. Thakur had claimed a wicket inadvertently to a plan that was not laid for him. That kind of defined Shardul Thakur the cricketer. He might not qualify as someone who 'makes things happen', but he sure has created his own unique niche as someone who 'somehow finds ways for things to happen for him'.

Arun reveals that India's strategy of bowling at middle or leg stump had to be altered for the bouncy track of the Gabba: 'We had to change our tactics for Brisbane. If you look at the mode of dismissals at the Gabba, it is generally edges to the keeper or the cordon. You hardly get any LBWs or bowleds, because to hit the top of the stumps you need to bowl so full that it almost becomes a half-volley, especially for bowlers that are not very tall . . . This was where a guy like Thakur was ideal, because his natural delivery was the outswinger. Plus, someone like Natarajan could keep angling the ball across the right-handers.'

The instructions to Thakur from Rahane were pretty straightforward: 'You'll have two slips in place constantly. And protection with a sweeper cover once the ball is old or the batsman is set. You just keep bowling your outswingers.'

For all the strategies India had conjured up, Rahane would have never imagined the only time the team had to vary their mode of attack it would be with a bowling unit that had a collective experience of four Tests. All he could do as captain now was hope for the best. Even with Washington, Rahane decided to play to the youngster's white-ball strengths rather than complicate matters. He might have come in as Ashwin's replacement, but there was no point in getting him to bowl like Ashwin.

'We didn't want to complicate things for Washi. We set a strong leg-side field and asked him to bowl a middle-stump line. His job was to build pressure with dot balls and not concede boundaries,' a senior member of the team would tell us later. 'It was like bowling in a T20 or ODI match, something he was very good at doing. So we decided, let's keep it simple and get him to execute a plan he was very comfortable with.'

The tactic worked for India and Washington. All three of his wickets in the first innings were of batters trying to force the issue and hit him off his consistent lines—Smith caught at mid-wicket,

Green bowled to a ball that pitched on middle stump and Lyon castled by a full delivery.

In spite of losing three wickets before lunch, Labuschagne would do what he does best at the Gabba: score another century. India had got the prolific right-hander to change his technique with their plans, and Labuschagne had, of course, accepted the challenge. He'd worked his backside off for hours on end, and this century was a deserved reward for those efforts.

But the incredibly inexperienced Indian attack never let the Aussies get away. They were, at best, a rookie welterweight, thrown into the ring against a super heavyweight. And yet, not only were they taking the blows without staggering even once, they were also landing a few on the slugger. With 369 on the board in their first innings, Australia, as many had believed, had once again been denied the chance of knocking this fragile Indian team out. Or at least bat them out of the game by posting a massive score, which has historically been the Aussie way of dominating Tests on home soil.

Much to the astonishment of the Australian commentators whom I was sharing the box with, and of every Australian tuned into this fascinating series, Rahane and his motley crew were simply not prepared to give up. And never did it seem more apparent than when Thakur and Washington came together on Day Two with India at 186/6.

★ ★ ★

'*Bhaaaat, kya batting kar raha hai yaar* (He's batting so well). He should be batting in the top four in domestic cricket. He is a genuine batsman.'

Washington's splendid stroke-play during the centre wicket practice sessions at Blacktown Oval, over the initial fourteen days of the tour, had certainly impressed Shastri. It was perhaps this first impression on tour that convinced the senior management that the left-hander could fit in at No. 7 once both Jadeja and Ashwin were ruled out.

With Ashwin not recovering in time post his Sydney Test heroics, Kuldeep Yadav was expected to be the logical choice. The left-arm wrist spinner had tasted success in Australia on the previous tour. In the pre-match show, the late great Shane Warne even went to the extent of saying that Kuldeep should be a certain starter and explained why the Gabba pitch would suit his protégé. But if Kuldeep was to be included as a direct swap for Ashwin, the batting would lack depth.

'With no Ash, we had to pick someone that could bat at number seven. Shardul could handle the bat at number eight. Washi was the only option,' one of the coaches told us. 'We couldn't take the risk of playing with three front-line pace bowlers and a spinner, given the pure workloads and fitness involved.'

This would be as good a time as any to talk up the amazing work that the Indian support staff had put in to keep ensuring that there were enough fit players for the visitors to field in Test after Test, even if by the end the cupboard went completely bare. That, too, while dealing with the constraints of bubble life and several other restrictions. For all the heroes that India found on the field, the physios, the masseurs and the strength and conditioning coaches deserve every supporting cast award that has come their way ever since.

'People had to realize that this tour came on the back of nine months of lockdown. No bowler had any game-time leading into the tour. Plus, the conditions in Brisbane were hot and steamy. We had to consider all those factors in our meeting with the team management,' one of the support staff explained to us.

The day before the match, Washington had a long batting session in the nets. The only problem for India was that there were no reserve bowlers left, except Tyagi. So he had to prepare to face Starc, Cummins and Hazlewood, with nothing more at his disposal than the throwdown specialists, who, by the way, also deserve a special mention for their efforts.

So, when Washington strode out, or rather ran, to the centre of the Gabba to face one of the most potent pace attacks in Test history, he was already swimming against the tide, only to be joined by Thakur soon after. A week earlier, the pair hadn't even had a set of white pads or white gloves in their kits. And the ones in use here had been borrowed from teammates. Here they were, with willow in hand, at the Gabba, a place from where those far superior to them had returned with bruised bodies and deflated egos.

But playing against boys much bigger than him was what Washington had done all his life. Since the time he was around six or seven. He would go to Marina Beach sitting in the backseat of his father's scooter, don his customized gloves and hit the ball so well that people would leave their weekend revelry and flock around to see him.

On Day Three at the Gabba, he had millions flocking to their TV sets to watch him cut, pull, drive, flick, duck and weave against Cummins & Co. That too on a surface the Aussie bowlers knew like the back of their hands. And some of the glorious punches down the ground told you why he had left an ever-lasting impression on Shastri.

If Washington was realizing his boyhood dream, Thakur was realizing his true calling while being at his feisty best. The third ball he faced from Cummins was hooked over fine leg for six. Thakur was never going to take a step back, and it was always going to be attack at all costs. But at the same time, there was plenty of application on show from this unlikely pair.

Those who know him well were not one bit surprised by how Thakur batted on that steamy Brisbane afternoon.

One of his state teammates reminisced about a Ranji Trophy match they played together: 'I remember Shardul volunteered to open the batting during that match. He was serious about opening. The coach at the time gave it a long thought as well, because there was no doubt that he was capable. He genuinely believed that he was capable of handling the new ball on a fresh pitch. There was so much conviction and a lot of us [Mumbai] guys had seen him score runs in difficult scenarios. That conviction is what makes him special.'

Thakur's cover drive on the up against Cummins symbolized the former's ability with the willow. According to some in the Indian dressing room, it was probably the shot of the series. *Shardulkar* even.

The 125-run partnership between the two pushed India to 336, only 33 runs behind Australia. Once again, they were back to going toe to toe with their bigger opponents. This battle was going into the final round.

By now, it wasn't just the former Aussie cricketers but even the Australian public who had started to warm up to this Indian team. Australia as a nation has always had a soft corner for an underdog on the sporting field. But rarely had they seen an underdog with such a big heart and such resilience on their shores.

It was a question we got asked wherever we went: 'How are they doing this? How are they not going down? How are they just wiping the blood off and getting back up for the fight?' And I must have spent many of my stints simply trying to find ways of telling people why. It included my theory on why I felt that this lot represented the 'brave new India' narrative more than any before them. Not only were they staying in the fight, but they were also doing so without having to conform to past narratives of 'having to beat Australia at their game'. It was like this team had, instead, opted for continuing to play their own game while beating Australia at theirs.

Going into the fourth day, there still seemed to be some who believed that Australia held all the aces and that the time had finally come for the hosts to show their Gabbatoir might. It didn't, in any way, lessen the awe that Rahane's team had already evoked around the country here. The Indian dressing room, however, had gone from a feeling of having 'nothing to lose' to possibly having 'everything to win'. It would have to start with showing that same discipline that had highlighted their several performances for one more day with the ball in hand—to stay proactive and keep taking wickets, rather than sit back and let Australia dictate terms.

Warner, unbeaten on 20 off 22 balls, was of course the big threat. The orders from Shastri and Arun were clear: 'No table tennis shots for Warner. Cut out the pull shots. Make him drive and get runs on the front foot.'

Warner and Harris began with scoring 32 runs from the first six overs. India had started to look shaky before a sharp Thakur bouncer rocked Harris as the opener fended awkwardly to glove the ball to the keeper.

Then it would be Siraj's turn to inspire his team again. He would run in hard while setting up and executing dismissals like a bowler playing in his fiftieth Test, knocking over both the well-set Labuschagne and Smith. Australia were throwing some hard punches, but India kept punching back.

At one point that afternoon, I was surprised to hear some of the Aussies in our commentary team talking about 'dangling the carrot' to the Indian team by declaring with a target of not more than 275. In their defence, the Indian top order hadn't given a great account of themselves in the first innings. I do remember responding to the umpteenth 'dangling carrot' remark with a line I wasn't proud of then, nor am I proud of it now. But like with those poor listeners on SEN, I think it's only fair that you endure it too: 'You dangle that carrot at this Indian team, they'll grab and turn it into the best carrot halwa they've ever had.' You be the judge.

India's resilience was, once again, winning over the Aussies on and off the field. It meant that the Australians had now lost their rhythm, especially when Cam Green continued to bat conservatively, and it was India controlling the pace of the game. Unprecedentedly so, considering the match scenario where the hosts were so far ahead.

It was to be Siraj's moment under the sun soon as he nabbed his fifth wicket and walked off the field holding the ball up with one hand while holding back tears as he looked at the heavens above. And nobody could have deserved it more. Nothing exemplified the unity within the team and the love for Siraj as the sight of Thakur, who was also looking for his fifth wicket, taking the catch and rushing towards Siraj with his arms raised, as if it was their shared moment of glory. In many ways, it was.

Shastri's words to Siraj—'You'll end up with a five-wicket haul in this Test series. Your father's *dua* [blessing] is with you'—had come true.

Dark clouds gathered over the Gabba as India prepared to start their run chase. The downpour that followed didn't last too long, but it stayed dark enough for the Indian openers to only have to face a couple of overs, much to the frustration of the Aussies, who kept remonstrating with the match officials. On a tour where so much had gone against them, it was perhaps only fair that, for once, the weather Gods were smiling on the visitors.

★ ★ ★

At some point during the Test, I had tweeted that if the Undertaker's Wrestlemania streak had finally ended, then so would the one that the Australian team had enjoyed at the Gabba. Someone on SEN had noticed it for sure. For as I waited to be introduced for the daily pre-match build-up show with the inimitable Gerard Whately and Peter Lalor, I was surprised to hear the voice of WWE's long-standing announcer Michael Cole from the final moments of Brock Lesnar's shock win in 2014, with these iconic words, 'Aaanndd, the streak is over.'

I was quick to note that it wasn't Lesnar that this Undertaker was up against at the Gabbatoir. It was, if anything, a battered and bruised cruiserweight at best, especially in terms of inexperience, trying to bring down the Phenom. My confidence in talking up India's chances even prompted wicketkeeping great and commentary colleague Ian Healy to challenge me to a friendly wager on air. We agreed to it too, even if only for a tiny sum. To his bemusement, I was ready to bet on India winning, not saving the Test. 'You are a brave man,' were his final words before the start of play.

Meanwhile at the Gabba, Rishabh Pant had walked out to the middle to get a view of the pitch. As Pant finished his inspection, he would tell a member of the Australian staff standing nearby, 'In India, you don't even see the pitch on Day Five. At least you can see the cracks on this one.'

As the Indian team gathered in a huddle for one last time on tour, the message from Rahane was simple: 'Whatever happens, let's smile and enjoy our last day together. Don't overthink it. We have come a long way and have terrific memories, so express yourself and remember to enjoy each moment.'

The coaching staff had set plans basically around a wait-and-assess approach. 'We decided that, let us get to lunch first and then re-evaluate. After that we can once again make an assessment at tea and so forth. Ravi then told them, "We are proud of you, and let's give it everything we have got today,"' Bharat Arun recalls now.

A couple of months before the series, Shubman Gill had spent hours getting accustomed to the bounce of Australian pitches by practising on a concrete pitch. When Shubman was a kid, his father would pay teenagers in the surrounding villages to hurl the ball on a 'cement' pitch from fifteen yards away to help him overcome his fear of a cricket ball. In some ways, he'd been preparing for his Gabba moment for nearly two decades. And right from the outset, you could sense that, regardless of the team plan, Gill had come out with one idea in his mind—to go for the target.

Though Rohit was dismissed cheaply, India, as always, had their insurance policy in Pujara at No. 3. As in Sydney, they could once again play to win at one end and play to draw at Pujara's end. The runs hadn't flowed off his willow on this Australia trip, but the respect for him among his peers had only continued to rise immensely. If Australia had witnessed Pujara the accumulator two years prior, this time around it was Pujara the prizefighter who'd landed on these shores.

Summing up Pujara's vital contribution, Arun said, 'Pujara is a very fierce competitor. He is like a territorial dog when it comes to defending his wicket. He didn't say anything, but his body language was such that he knew he had a bigger role to play in the series. They had better fields for Pujara. They also knew he doesn't loft the ball, so they never had a long off or long on.

'In spite of not scoring freely, he occupied the crease. He had a slightly different role . . . With all the injuries happening, we needed his experience to wear down the Aussie attack. Pujara being there bearing the brunt of the attack would mean batting was getting easier at the other end after forty overs or so.'

India still needed 244 runs to get at the first interval, but Gill and Pujara had looked largely untroubled. In the Indian dressing room, there was no major discussion, only a few encouraging words.

There was a sense of desperation building in the Australian camp, though, as in Sydney. That very visible crack that ran right along the pitch wasn't of any use to them. The first session was an extended one, and with the ball close to forty overs old, some members of their coaching staff felt it was time for Plan B.

'In hindsight, we could have been more patient and stuck to a simple plan of bowling in the channel with the odd bumper. Players like Gill, thrive when runs start to flow. To be honest, we hadn't bowled too badly in the first session, we just didn't get the breakthrough. Plus, India were only scoring at 2.5 runs per over, so in a way we were applying pressure. But there were others in the dressing room that felt we needed to change,' a member of the Aussie camp told me.

Australia's Plan B was to start a bumper barrage. The over before lunch, Gill had upper-cut Starc for a six over third man, so India had a glimpse of what might be coming after lunch. One member of the coaching staff had even briefly asked Gill to be mindful of the plan. Gill's response was that of a man who had already chalked out a solution.

'He had observed that one side of the boundary was shorter, and it was less risky to hit towards that end. He was very clear about which length he could pull from and which length he had to duck,' said Arun.

The first seven overs after lunch proved that Gill knew what he was talking about as India added 43 runs to their total. This was where, as the Aussies would later admit, the plot was lost for Australia—especially in the over where the young Indian opener tore into Starc.

With Gill gone, all eyes turned to Rahane. How Rahane would approach his innings, you felt, would set the tone for the rest of the day. Rahane pulled the second ball he faced from Hazlewood well in front of square. One of the Australian commentators on Channel 7 immediately asked Ricky Ponting, 'Well, is the chase on?' An over or so later, as Rahane launched Lyon over the deep-midwicket fence, you knew the chase was indeed on.

'We had decided that one of us had to keep moving the game forward. I didn't want Pujara to change the way he was playing. He was so comfortable doing what he was doing—occupying the crease. So I thought, instead of asking Puji to change, I would take the game on,' Rahane would explain later.

This was Rahane the leader, the captain, the team man. His breezy 24 from 22 balls was just the fillip India needed. As Pant and Pujara walked off at tea, India still required 145 runs with seven wickets in hand.

★ ★ ★

This is Bharat Arun setting the scene up for arguably India's finest hour as a Test team away from home: 'At tea, Rishabh was in the loo, and he was telling Gill, "In the next 5–7 overs, once we reach the score of 200, I will go after the bowling, and once those initial runs come, they will also panic." Ravi overheard this conversation and came out to let me know about it. He wanted to know what we should tell Rishabh. We thought about it and said, Let's leave them alone. If he really gets it, he gets it. So far it has been an outstanding tour. Let's take whatever result comes. We have prepared them for these situations, and if they are being fearless, then let's not stop them. We may even end up losing the Test match, but with that kind of effort, having come so close to winning the Test also would have been a moral victory for us.

'Nothing succeeds like success. Winning is a totally different perspective, but if you run after victories, maybe that can eat you up. The pressure of going for victory can eat you up. So that's why we just left them and didn't put any thoughts or ideas in their head after tea.'

So Pant had decided that there was only one way out—to go for the win.

His presence at the crease meant Australia was once again in a dilemma: Do they attack or defend? Lyon kept bowling around the wicket and wide of the off stump to lure Pant into a false stroke, similar to the one he had played on Day Five in Sydney. Pant was happy to play the waiting game as he offered no shot to a series of balls.

'Lyon was enticing him with that line. Lyon thought he had got him out twice. He was aware of it, and Ravi had told him about it. Rishabh had told us, "If he keeps bowling like that, I will let it go." Somewhere, the real Rishabh had to come through, and it was only a matter of time before he charged down the track and smashed him over long on. We could almost hear him go, "*Mere area me tha toh maar diya* (He was in my area, so I hit him),"' Arun recalled with a chuckle.

Shastri was impressed with Pant's balance of aggression and defence, but it would be the left-hander's shot selection that would leave the Indian coach extremely satisfied.

Shastri and Pant had had a chat about shot selection after Pant's dismissal for 97 in Sydney. The head coach wasn't disappointed with Pant taking on Lyon, but he felt Pant needed to be a smarter about it:

'Why are you playing that shot [lofting him over cover]? You play the reverse sweep against fast bowling. Why don't you reverse him instead? The field and the line he is bowling is ideal for you to reverse. If there is a sweeper on the off side in front of square, then play the reverse sweep. If they put fielders in those traditional spots, hit him somewhere else—which is also your strength.'

Rishabh replied with, '*Ye tareeka bohot achha hai* (This advice is brilliant). If you tell me don't do it, I will do it. But, sir, you have given a different option, and I will try it.'

While Pant carried on doing what he does at his end, Pujara was doing what he does best at his. He was giving nothing away to the Aussies. As in Sydney, they'd seemingly given up on dismissing their nemesis and, instead, were trying to bully him out. It only made Pujara more determined. Those steely eyes got sterner and more focused with every blow. And every time he was struck on some part of his body—and by the end there were marks everywhere—it only convinced him that the pain was worth it. Pujara was going nowhere. Like in the case of Ashwin and Vihari in Sydney, this was a display of fearlessness and courage that will go into the folklore of Indian cricket and stay there forever.

India would lose another couple of wickets, including that of Pujara, to the second new ball. When Washington strode out to join Pant, India still needed another 63 runs from 13.2 overs. The thought of whether India should look for a draw might have crossed the minds of a few in the Indian dressing room, but they were having none of it. Not with Pant holding the fort.

'We can't change anything now. You can't ask them to play for a draw, because that will put the Aussies on top. If he plays in his own style and scores runs, the pressure stays on the Aussies,' Arun recalls thinking at the time.

As the target came down below 50, it was obvious that there would be only two results possible. Pant had taken the draw out of the equation. And the moment Washington pulled Cummins over fine leg for a six, the Indian dressing room felt that it was the Australians who had well and truly started to panic. It showed on the field too. Paine's wicketkeeping, once again, was getting scrappier. There had been one more missed stumping earlier in the session off Lyon's bowling.

As the target reduced to single figures, even Rahane, the calmest man in the dressing room, who had never lost his nerve throughout the whole campaign, began to feel anxious.

'It was the only time I felt my emotions could take over. But there was Rohit next to me, saying, "We are doing this, yaar." This allowed me to keep my emotions in check. I just took a deep breath, and just soaked in each ball as we came closer and closer to the target,' Rahane said.

Even the late drama of losing Washington and Thakur in quick succession wasn't going to affect that all-pervading confidence, especially with Pant at the crease.

Finally, the moment arrived as Pant drove Josh Hazlewood towards the mid-off boundary past the shadows of the mighty Gabba. The curtain had finally dropped on one of the most astonishing comebacks ever witnessed on a sporting field. But along the way, courtesy of Pant's audacity with bat in hand, he had made sure that this Indian team would be looked at with a sense of awe never witnessed before.

It was Indian cricket's greatest moment of glory. It was perhaps Indian cricket's most famous Test win. It was arguably the most memorable Test rubber of all time. It was a day's play that will be replayed for years to come, not just in India but all around the globe.

I was asked to join the call on SEN, with less than 10 runs left to win, to sum up the final few moments of India's victory and the celebrations that followed. And I thankfully managed to find the right words to put it into context. I spoke about belief, pride and the magnitude of what these bunch of unlikely heroes had pulled off by marching into Australia's fortress and bringing it down piece by piece. I could hear Ian Healy getting a bit emotional as he agreed with me on this being the ultimate comeback story in Test history. Unfortunately for me, we both forgot about our bet in that moment. But it was a sign of how this Indian team had not only won their own fans over like never before but had also swept even the most hard-nosed of Aussies off their feet.

★ ★ ★

The Indian players ran on to the field and embraced each other. There were celebrations all around India. As the visitors walked over to shake hands with the Australians, Rahane saw disappointment in Lyon's face and heard a few Australian players say to Lyon, 'Sorry, Gazza, we couldn't do it for you.' It was supposed to be the off-spinner's special occasion after all, playing his hundredth Test.

Rahane immediately got an India shirt and got all the players to sign it before he headed out for the post-match presentation. It would take the Indians close to an hour and a half to return to the dressing room. 'There were so many Indian fans, and we just wanted to live the moment on the ground. The mind was blank, we really didn't have any words. All our actions post the match were spontaneous. We just wanted to be side by side looking at that Indian flag,' said Arun.

One of the first people Rahane sought out as they walked back in was Kuldeep Yadav. The left-arm spinner had been a part of the squad from the day they had landed but had only featured in couple of the white-ball matches. Rahane's words were loud, so that everyone could hear him, and went something along the lines of: 'You are equally a part of this journey. Don't ever feel like you weren't. You have played your role, and like some of us, you are part of a team that has beaten Australia twice at home.' Having been the twelfth man for fourteen consecutive matches before making his Test debut himself, Rahane knew what it must have been like to be Kuldeep.

Around the same time, Tim Paine pulled Lyon aside in the Australian dressing room to apologize to him because he felt like he'd 'let him down' with his wicketkeeping and his captaincy. 'People will see your numbers in the series and think you had a struggle, but it's on me, and I let you down. If I'd kept up to my standards, your figures would have been different,' Paine is learnt to have said.

* * *

'One thing that stood out for me was how none of the players rushed to their phones. We all sat around, talked and celebrated. It was defining because in the era we live in, the first thing we want to do is to go to our phones, but the fact that we just wanted to continue living that moment was just amazing,' said Arun, setting the scene for us once again, this time in the dressing room.

It was two and half hours later that the team returned to the hotel. And we could tell how emotional both the captain and coach were during the final press conference.

When Gaurav spoke to Thakur that night, the latter's voice was croaky. Asked if it was due to all the yelling or celebrating, his reply was, 'No, it's from all the pickle juice I've had to consume to stop cramping, as I was on the field for such a long time. It was also the humid conditions throughout the tour.'

As the team assembled at the hotel to begin their celebrations, they received a call from Virat Kohli congratulating them on an epic win. They had managed to do exactly what the captain had felt was achievable in Dubai, beating a full-strength Australia with Smith and Warner back.

'Great things have been achieved when you hit rock bottom. Looking back, it was the belief of the players at teatime that made us feel we had done a good job as coach. A lot of people talk about process but not many can define it,' Arun told me.

Shastri remained extremely emotional the following morning when he spoke to us: 'They can never take this away from me. We have achieved the unbelievable. I sit here thinking I have accomplished everything in cricket. I have been involved with this great game for close to fifty years, but this is the best feeling I have had. F**k, to beat the Aussies in their backyard, not once but f***ing twice. I could not be prouder of this team,' he said, or something to that effect.

But as Arun recalls, the real extent of their achievement only hit home once they landed in Dubai airport, where they were received by hundreds of Indian fans. 'That was when it dawned upon us. It was a six-hour halt and Ravi and I can both tell you that the drink tasted the best only then as we began to realize what we had done as a team.'

★ ★ ★

There will be many great matches and great series that'll get played all around the world. This Indian team will be a part of many of those too. They already have been perhaps by the time you read this book. But you can be rest assured that there will never be a series like what we witnessed during the incredible Australian summer of 2020–21.

Maybe because it was, in the end, more than a victory on the cricket field. It was a triumph of the human spirit. It was a lesson that, however bleak your prospects may seem, there is always a way to overcome even the most imposing of challenges placed before you. You just need to find the will to do so, like Rahane & Co. did. That it happened in the midst of one of the deadliest pandemics our world has ever seen only added to the sense of hope and belief that was provided by this remarkable Indian cricket team.

I wonder if we'll ever come to grips with the magnitude of what they actually achieved down under between November 2020 and January 2021, if it'll ever quite fully sink in. It probably is like a movie script that you'll never tire of going back to. For, you'll always discover a new hero or a moment to get inspired by. But every time you do, one part of you will wonder if it really happened. If you really were there when India redeemed the unredeemable in Melbourne, when they saved the unsavable in Sydney, and when they dominated the indomitable in Brisbane. If I really was there when Ajinkya Rahane and his team scripted the greatest epic in Indian cricket history and, in turn, became Indian cricket's miracle makers.

Acknowledgements

I met Gaurav 'Gav' Joshi for the first time a decade ago in a cricket press box, not surprisingly. I wasn't really taken by his accent but immediately was in awe of his passion and knowledge for cricket. In addition to how seamlessly he had made the move from the IT universe to our big, bad world of cricket journalism.

I don't think I have spoken more to anyone else on the phone ever since that first meeting. It's not always about cricket, but it somehow comes back to it. After all, we spent a month and a half travelling in a campervan around England without having to turn on the radio even once. We certainly didn't need to during the two months we were gallivanting around Australia, covering India's unforgettable tour down under.

And there was no way I would have gone ahead with writing this book without Gav being a major part of it. It also gave me the chance to share the writing journey with one of my closest friends.

Gav is the kind of friend everyone dreams of having in their life. Someone who's there for you unconditionally, but also someone who always listens. A true mate's mate. He owes all these wonderful qualities, of course, to his wonderful dad and mom, Vijay and Manasi Joshi, who, apart from being generous and giving to a fault to all comers, define and embellish the label of being 'supportive parents'. They housed me on plenty of occasions during that crazy summer and made me feel at home like only they can.

I'd better also make a mention of my mother here in the acknowledgements, to avoid getting into trouble when I see her next. And of my wife, Isha, for having put up with my madness for ten years and counting. Thanks also to Donna and Gerald, on the other side of my fence, for ensuring that Adelaide became our forever home.

I'm so thankful to Ganesh Chandrasekharan, who opened the doors to Australia for me by offering me the super gig with Cricbuzz, the No. 1 cricket website that he runs so efficiently as editor.

I wouldn't be able to say how grateful I am to Adam Collins, for discovering the commentator in me before even I did, and to Gerard Whateley and Mitchell Scott, for all the support and opportunities that have come my way on radio ever since. It was both an honour and a privilege to share the box with some cricketing legends and to enjoy the unique vantage point that radio provides to soak in the drama.

Thanks to the two brilliant cricket teams for producing a series that will never be replicated or matched. From the Australian fast bowlers' breathtaking exploits in Adelaide to R. Ashwin's classical battles with Steve Smith and Marnus Labuschagne, from Cheteshwar Pujara's resistance and Ajinkya Rahane's leadership to Rishabh Pant's daredevilry and Prithi Ashwin braving the Covid protocols to support her husband and keep her kids entertained . . .

Thanks to Ravi Shastri and Bharat Arun, for always being open and honest with their discussions and for enriching our understanding of the extraordinary challenges posed by this tour, and the highs and lows of being in charge of an Indian team. To the amazing health professionals around Australia who somehow allowed for this tour to take place, despite the many sacrifices they had to make while dealing with the Covid chaos.

I wouldn't have become an author if not for Radhika Marwah, my commissioning editor and dear friend, who pushed me to write books and has stuck with me despite the stress and anxiety that I bring to her life.

A lot of gratitude, as always, to Australia, the best country to live in and to drive around. You really are a *fu$@ing* beauty.

And finally, to the game of cricket, for giving me a second chance in life. I wouldn't have been around, and certainly not where I am, if it weren't for you standing by me.